THE Memory DOCTOR

FUN, SIMPLE

TECHNIQUES

TO IMPROVE

MEMORY &

BOOST YOUR

BRAIN POWER

DOUGLAS J. MASON, PSY.D., LCSW
AND SPENCER XAVIER SMITH

NEW HARBINGER PUBLICATIONS, INC.

Distributed in Canada by Raincoast Books

Copyright © 2005 by Douglas Mason and Spencer Smith
New Harbinger Publications, Inc.
5674 Shattuck Avenue
Oakland, CA 94609

Cover design by Amy Shoup
Text design by Michele Waters-Kermes
Acquired by Catharine Sutker

ISBN 1-57224-370-8 Paperback

All Rights Reserved

Printed in the United States of America

New Harbinger Publications' Web site address: www.newharbinger.com

07   06   05

10 9 8 7 6 5 4 3 2 1

First printing

This book is dedicated to my daughters Stephanie, Jenna and Jordyn, my wife Brenda and my parents Ray and Mable.

—DJM

For Marie and Tristan.

—SS

Contents

Introduction

I got up this morning at four A.M. to get some writing done before heading out to the hospital. As usual, I started by putting a cup of coffee into the microwave to heat it up for the adventure at hand. I sat down at my computer and started writing about memory. After struggling through a few lines I decided I needed my java to fuel my creative juices, but where was it? I looked everywhere. I went into the bathroom, the living room, and the kitchen. I searched the pantry and the porch. Try as I might, I just couldn't seem to locate my coffee. After ten minutes or so I remembered where I'd put it. Actually, I didn't remember, I was reminded when I saw the microwave.

What a farce! A neuropsychologist sitting down to write about memory unable to find his morning fix. Am I becoming senile? Is it just a matter of time until I descend into the depths of Alzheimer's as my grandmother and her mother did? My God, what else have I forgotten lately? Okay, hold on. First of all, it was four A.M. I'd had about four hours of sleep the previous night and probably less the night before that. I was thinking about the ten patients who would be waiting for me at the hospital that day and what time I needed to leave to meet my first appointment. I was distracted by the cat scratching at the door to come in, and the baby starting to stir in the next room. As for the coffee, well, I suspect that if I'd had a cup of coffee before losing my coffee, then I probably wouldn't have lost my coffee.

This pattern of forgetfulness is a normal one. We have only so much cognitive energy that we can expend at any given moment, and at four A.M. on that particular morning the energy expenditure necessary for my multitasking far exceeded my daybreak cognitive resources. To forget is normal; to forget that you forgot is not. In other words, as long as you keep remembering that you forgot, you are going to be okay.

THE WARDEN OF THE BRAIN

Shakespeare called memory "the warden of the brain," charged with keeping watch over our personal history of being. Should this sentry begin to fail, your own record of self can become endangered. We identify ourselves so completely with our memory that even the slightest glitch in our ability to remember can cause great fear, even panic.

Who would you be if your record of self was stripped from you? If the vast complex of memories that make up your life—your first kiss, falling in love with your partner, graduating from college, your first real job, the birth of your children—if all these things were to drop down the memory well never to be seen again, who would you be? What would it mean about you? More to the point, what does it mean that you have started to regularly forget where your keys are? Does it mean that you are in the early stages of Alzheimer's disease and soon you will be lost in a world without memories?

The answer is simple—probably not. If you were browsing at a bookstore and ran across this book, or if you were perusing the selections online, and decided that your memory did indeed need improvement, you haven't started to lose your record of self. The truth is that this fear is unfounded. Even people with severe dementia do not completely lose their identity. Moreover, if you are reading this page right now, then you are far from that level of debilitation. So relax, take a deep breath, and read this book. You aren't "losing your mind"; you just can't remember where you put the keys. We can help you with that.

HOW THIS BOOK WILL HELP YOU

Perhaps you are starting to have "senior moments," and for the first time in your life you are forgetting things you've never forgotten before. Or perhaps you are so busy that you just can't remember all the things you have to do in the day. Maybe you are someone who's "never had a good memory," or perhaps you've picked up this book because you feel that your memory can use a little boost. Whatever your reason, you have picked up this book because your memory is important to you and you want some help to make it work better.

As Shakespeare suggested, memory is, in fact, intimately linked to who we are. The record of our lives that we keep in memory comprises the acts in the play that led up to the scene we are in today. These memories define us. They tell us who we are and remind us of where we came from.

These kinds of memories, however, are not the types of memories that we will deal with in this book. This is not a book about defining your memories or exploring what your memory has to tell you about yourself. *The Memory Doctor* will not prescribe ways to cope with memories of your past. Rather, what this book will teach you is how to remember where you put your keys in the morning when the baby was crying and you were already late for work.

This is a book about improving your memory. In this book we will give you eight easy-to-follow chapters guaranteed to help you outwit your "senior moments" and sharpen your memory to such a degree that your friends and colleagues will be left in awe.

This book is also not like those television infomercial programs that promise to teach even the most monkey-minded how to master the incredible skill of remembering the name of every person in the room while simultaneously keeping track of a list of fifty random numbers. What this book promises is far more practical. We will leave recalling memories of the past to therapists and memorizing nonsensical trivia to TV wizards.

What *The Memory Doctor* offers is a way to improve the quality of your life by improving the quality of your memory about the things that make a difference to you. As far as we are concerned, this is really the key. Many different people will come to this book for many different reasons. The one reason you all have in common is that all of you want to improve your memory because, in some way, your memory (or lack thereof) has begun to have a negative impact on the quality of your life.

Forgetting where you put your keys is a pain in the butt. Forgetting where you parked your car is even worse. And forgetting the name of your best friend's new wife can be a social disaster. Maybe you are frightened because you were a half hour late to pick up your kid from soccer practice because you forgot, or perhaps your boss is angry with you because you were supposed to file some paperwork with the PR office two weeks ago, and you completely spaced it.

Whatever your reason, this book is for you. In these pages you will learn how to remember these kinds of things more easily and much, much more. *The Memory Doctor* will help you forget how to forget and remember how to remember. *The Memory Doctor* will . . . Before this turns into a carnival spiel, let's take a sip of coffee and teach you how to use this book.

HOW TO USE THIS BOOK

As we've already said, this book is divided into eight chapters. Basically, you can read these chapters in any old order you like. If you choose to read from beginning to end (the recommended way of reading books), you will end up with a pretty good overview of how your memory works (chapter 1); the specific memory areas you may be having problems with and these ways to improve it (chapter 2); techniques for accomplishing your goals (chapters 3 to 5 and 8); how medications and supplements can affect your memory for better or worse (chapters 6 and 7); and the directions memory research is moving in today (conclusion).

If you choose to skip around from chapter to chapter, we would recommend that, at the very least, you read through chapters 1 and 2 completely. These two chapters are pretty important. In chapter 1 you will find an overview of the way that your memory works and the different types of memory you can put to use. This information is an important foundation for the rest of the book.

It may be that the single best way you can influence your memory function is to have a clear idea as to how memory works, and then actually pay attention to the workings of your own memory. Because remembering is second nature for most of us, we don't really think about how memory works. As such, we lose sight of how we can improve our memory. The material in chapter 1 provides a way out of this ignorance.

Chapter 2 will help you set goals for improving your memory. This is the chapter that will help you personalize this material. If you don't have a clear idea as to the types of memory problems you are experiencing, it will be very difficult for you to get a grip on what you need to do to change. Setting precise goals for your memory will help you get the most out of this book and ultimately the most out of your memory.

After reading the first two chapters, do whatever you want. If you are particularly interested in the chapter on supplements, by all means read it immediately. There is nothing to stop you from doing this. Or if you would rather hurl the book out the window, do that. It will do nothing to improve your memory and will be a waste of your money, but it may be a good tension release.

In all seriousness, there is some good science in this book, and there are ways that have been proven effective time and time again to change memory for the better. Some of them are as old as the hills (like tying a string around your finger), but most of them reflect the most recent and relevant research that has been done in this field.

Our understanding of how the brain works has increased so dramatically in the last ten years that, in some ways, our old models of brain function have become completely outdated. For example, you may have learned while growing up that you have a given, finite amount of brain cells (neurons) at birth, that these neurons cannot ever be regenerated, and that, over time, your brain slowly "dies." You also may have learned that once neural networks are destroyed, they can never be reestablished. This information has all turned out to be false.

The human brain is a much more complex, pliable, malleable, regenerating organ than was thought possible. The brain has more in common with a muscle than was imagined twenty years ago. And, like a muscle, training and exercising the brain can provide extraordinary results.

We hold the human mind, and particularly the functions of memory, in scientifically appropriate awe. The one idea we hope you will take away from this book more than anything else is this: Your mind and your memory are limited only by the efforts you put into expanding them. Our hope is that you will use this book to help you expand your mind and your memory, improve the quality of your life, and have a little fun along the way.

> YOUR MIND AND YOUR MEMORY ARE LIMITED ONLY BY THE EFFORTS YOU PUT INTO EXPANDING THEM.

1

Memory: An Overview

I n our culture we tend to refer to memory somewhat loosely. Every day, wherever you are, you can hear phrases like "Remember when . . ." or "You have such a good memory." In these general terms, memory can mean anything from the cumulative life experiences of a particular individual to the neurochemical interactions that occur in the brain that record those experiences.

In fact, in some ways the concept of memory can be seen as a metaphor. It suggests a fixed, tangible set of information all stored in one place that can be accessed at will. We tend to think that our minds work the way that computers do, but nothing could be further from the truth. In fact, different kinds of memories are stored in different parts of the brain. Because the human brain is such a complex, sophisticated organ, human memory is actually an incredibly complex, dynamic event. To help you get some perspective on this, we would like to start out by breaking apart what we call "memory" into its different components.

Most of the time we take our memory for granted. We tend to think of it as a psychological process that happens beyond our control. But when you break memory into its different components, you start to see very specific places in your memory where you can actively make a difference.

THE PROCESS OF MEMORY

The first thing you need to understand is that there is a process by which you remember information. In simple terms, you put information into your brain, it stays in there for a while, and you get it back out later. There are names for these three distinct stages in the memory process. They are encoding (putting information in), storage (keeping the information in there), and retrieval (getting the information back out again). But before going into too much detail about these areas, let's start out with an example we can use as a reference point for exploring the three different stages of memory.

ROCK 'N' ROLL MADNESS:
A MODEL FOR MEMORY

Suppose one sunny afternoon you are standing in your kitchen washing the dishes. You have the radio on and you're listening to a new song, one you have never heard before. While you run the sponge over the plate again and again, watching your lovely skin wrinkling into the prunelike texture of dishpan hands, you notice that you've started humming along with the radio. Soon enough you're singing along with the chorus every time it rolls around. By the end of the song, you're holding a wooden spoon in your hand like a microphone, and you're dancing around the kitchen belting out the lyrics, pretending you're on a stage, and hoping that nobody walks in on you. The song ends, your performance closes, and you finish your dishes.

Later in the day you drive to the grocery store to pick up a couple of things for dinner and you start singing the song again. People in the neighboring cars look at you strangely, but you don't care. You rip out the chorus a couple of times at the stoplight, and when the light turns, you slam down the accelerator and zoom off into the sunset, or rather, toward the grocery store parking lot.

What happened here besides a short bout of madness driven by rock 'n' roll? It's fairly evident that you remembered the song, but it's the process by which you remembered it that we want to explore in a little more detail.

ENCODING

The first stage of the memory process is called *encoding*. While you were listening to the song, your mind was taking in raw auditory data (the lyrics and the music) and turning it into a code (a set of neural networks) to store the information for later use. Once you realized that you liked the song, you probably started paying more attention to it. This helped you to encode the information more deeply in your brain. (Later on, you will

> ## GOOD ENCODING LEADS TO GOOD MEMORY.

learn the vital importance of paying attention to the encoding process; see chapter 4). Soon you were singing along with the song. This rehearsal (repeating the same thing again and again until it is firmly stored) helped the encoding process embed the song even deeper into your mind. (You will learn more about rehearsal in chapter 5).

Encoding is the point of entry for information to be held in memory. If nothing were ever encoded, nothing could ever be remembered. It is also the stage of your memory that you can have the greatest influence on. Good encoding leads to good memory. If the information is not encoded well, there will be no way for you to recall it effectively. Becoming conscious about the way that you encode information will take you a long way to improving your memory. Much of this book will provide you with strategies to improve your encoding.

STORAGE

Let's go back to the song you were singing. After the song on the radio was over, you stopped singing and went back to the dishes. However, at that point the song was already stored in your memory. That's why you were able to sing it later in your car.

Most people who worry about their memory problems are worrying about their ability to store information. That is, they seem to think that somehow the information that was stored will be lost, or that they will lose their ability to retain information. Ironically, this is the memory stage that is almost never affected in any significant way. Even Alzheimer's patients do not lose their ability to store information completely. This is due, in part, to the fact that the way in which our brains store information is so complex.

Memories are not stored in one particular place in the brain. In fact, your memories are a vast array of neural networks spread out all over your brain. A memory of any single event is tied in this way to many different systems in your brain. For example, when you were singing you were also washing the dishes. This means that the memory of the song will in some way be tied to doing dishes. In fact, you may find yourself remembering the song the next time you do the dishes. The memory is also tied to the feeling of your wrinkled dishpan hands. These kinds of ties are one reason that the encoding process is so important. The more energy that is put into encoding, the stronger and more complex these neural networks will be.

WORKING MEMORY

It can be useful to think about your ability to store information as a twofold process. The first storage tank that information is dumped into is your working memory (also known as "short-term memory"). Your *working memory* is all of the information that you need to do a task in any given moment.

Let's say you want to call a record shop to find out if they have that song you were just listening to. You look up the number for the store and then deposit that phone number into your working memory. Assuming that you haven't spent too much time trying to remember the number and that you have no compelling reasons to keep it in your memory, the information will simply be discarded after your need for it ends.

If, on the other hand, you do decide to memorize it, and you say the number to yourself over and over again (rehearsal), it will soon be transferred to your long-term memory. Your *long-term memory* is the accumulation of all the things you have stored in your mind, and it is quite vast.

As mentioned earlier, the capacity your mind has to store information is almost never affected in any significant way. So rest assured, if you are having a hard time remembering things, your brain isn't broken. You don't need to repair your storage facilities. It will be much more to your benefit to concentrate on your encoding and retrieval processes.

RETRIEVAL

The process of retrieving a memory is the place where most people will notice a problem. Let's say, for example, that instead of rocking out to the song in your car on the way to the store, you had a different kind of experience. Suppose you kept thinking about the song; the lyrics were on the tip of your tongue, but you just couldn't seem to remember them. This would be a problem in the retrieval stage of your memory. *Retrieval* is the process by which we get information back out of storage.

There are things that you can do to improve your ability to retrieve information, and lots of them will be reviewed in this book. Still, you should be aware that most retrieval problems are really problems with encoding. That is to say, if the information had been encoded better in the first place, it is unlikely that you would have a hard time retrieving it. So, although there are ways to improve your retrieval, the part of your memory that you really want to concentrate on is encoding.

WORKING THE MEMORY MUSCLE

Throughout this book we will give you little exercises to help you put some of the concepts you will find here into practice. If you want to improve your memory, these exercises are your chance to do that. More and more, neuropsychologists are beginning to understand that the mind is like a muscle. If you put it to work, it will improve. If you allow it to languish, it will get out of shape. The more effort you put into improving your memory, the more likely you are to get results.

This doesn't mean that you should spend night and day doing memory exercises. If you do, soon you will find that you are wasting your life. Just keep it real. Put the concepts in this book into practice as much as feels comfortable to you. There is no need to wear yourself out (in fact, if you do, it is actually less likely that your memory will improve). Be diligent, but don't be lazy. Now, let's try the first exercise.

MAKING IT WORK: Encoding

The next time you want to remember something, think about your encoding process while you are trying to remember it. Let's say you always lose your keys. The next time you put them down, think to yourself, "I am now encoding the placement of my keys." Go ahead and say it aloud. If you are surrounded by judgmental people who will think you've lost your mind for saying such a thing aloud, simply tell them, "I am working on my memory, and it would serve you well to do the same." After all, this is your memory we are talking about here.

Be conscious about what is going on in your brain. Think about the neural networks being formed when you put your keys on the table. Look at your keys for a little while and make sure that their placement is ingrained in your memory.

TYPES OF MEMORY

There are basically two different types of memory: The stuff you know you know, and the stuff you know, but you don't know you know. These are often referred to as declarative and non-declarative memory, respectively.

Declarative memory is conscious memory. It is knowledge of facts and events that includes both *episodic* (time-related data of past experiences) and *semantic* (fact-related) data. Declarative memory stores information about facts (who, what, when, where, how, and why) and the relationships between them. Other terms that you may hear associated with declarative memory might include "explicit memory" or "cognitive memory." It is this kind of memory that most people are referring to when they say they have begun to notice lapses in their memory.

Declarative memory is any information that you can readily call to hand at any time. This could include a friend's birthday, a telephone number, directions to your favorite shopping mall, or the periodic table of elements (assuming that you have such a thing memorized). It is the sum total of your intellectual knowledge.

Nondeclarative memory is memory that cannot be accessed consciously. It includes motor learning, habits, and conditioning. Nondeclarative memory includes the skills achieved through repetition, such as driving a car or riding a bike. It involves multiple senses and systems and utilizes multiple motor and cognitive pathways in its execution. Other names for nondeclarative memory include "implicit memory," "dispositional memory," or "nonconscious memory."

The functional purpose for drawing this distinction between these two types of memory is so that you can more easily recognize the areas in your life where you can make improvements. It's unlikely that you will have a big impact on your nondeclarative memory. You can, however, make a big difference in your declarative memory. There are two major subtypes of declarative memory that we will explore here: verbal memory and visual memory.

Are You a Painter or a Singer?

It's likely you are already somewhat aware of the differences between verbal and visual memory. And it's also likely that you have an implicit knowledge of where your strengths and weaknesses lie. However, you may not be using your strengths to their full effect. So, let's begin with a brief exploration of the differences between verbal and visual memory.

VERBAL MEMORY

Verbal memory is the ability to remember data that relates to words. If you are the type of person who is likely to pick up that wooden spoon and start singing when you hear a song you know or love, the likelihood is that you have a strong verbal memory. People with good verbal memories tend to read a lot, memorize poetry, and prefer written instructions to maps. If you think of yourself more as a singer than a painter, you are probably a more verbally oriented person.

VISUAL MEMORY

Visual memory, on the other hand, is the ability to store visually oriented data. If you are a visually oriented person, the notion of singing along with the radio while working in the kitchen may not appeal to you at all. Perhaps the song would be more likely to inspire you to paint a picture on your walls. If you love to look at fine art, see the shape of road signs more quickly than the words written on them, and pay more attention to the scenery in a movie than to the characters' dialogue, it is likely that you are a visually oriented person. These are the painters, not the singers.

Of course, these are only personal inclinations. Verbal and visual memory are not at all mutually exclusive, and it may be that you love fine art and you memorize poetry. The idea here is to become more conscious of your own orientation. Most people tend to be either more visual or more verbal. By figuring out where you are on the spectrum, you can start to put your strengths to use for yourself. The reason for this is quite simple—most information can be stored in either a visual or a verbal fashion.

TRANSLATING VISUAL AND VERBAL INFORMATION

People translate verbal information to visual information and vice versa every day without even realizing it. In fact, like so many events associated with memory, making these translations is such a natural process that we lose sight of its value. However, if you want to improve your memory, it is helpful to be aware of these translations of information and consciously put them to use for yourself.

To illustrate this process with an ordinary example, consider how you would find your way to a department store (or anywhere else for that matter). Let's say you are in desperate need of a wool cap. Winter has just started, and your ears freeze every time you go outside. You decide to go to the local department store, but you are new to the area and you aren't sure where it is. So, you go online and get directions from one of the mapping services. You will notice that most of these services offer directions in two ways—written verbal instructions and maps. If you are a visual learner, you will likely use the map. If you are a verbal learner, you will choose the written instructions.

But let's say that you can't find this particular shopping mall online and you must call the store for directions. You talk to a clerk there and she gives you verbal instructions that you write down. If you are a visual learner, this is going to pose a bit of a problem. What would you do? Of course, most visual learners will go and get their handy-dandy street map and figure out the way to the store with the map.

This is the very essence of translating between verbal and visual information: Taking a set of verbal information and turning it into visual data or taking a set of visual data and turning it into verbal information. These translation techniques can be very useful tools for you as you start to explore new ways to improve your memory. If you are a visual learner, translate information into visual data for yourself. In this way, you will be storing information in parts of your brain that are already very strong, and you will find it much easier to remember that information.

There is almost no limit to the ways that you can translate between these two types of memory. Just get creative. If you have a hard time remembering your best friend's hamster's name (verbal information), try thinking of that cute little hamster face (visual information) when you think of the name. If you always forget where you put your shoes and you have a strong verbal memory, you might say to yourself when you take them off, "I am leaving my shoes next to the washing machine." Or, if you are a visually oriented individual, try placing a picture in your mind of the washing machine with your shoes right next to it.

MAKING IT WORK:
Verbal and Visual Memory

Try it. The next time you want to remember something, try using your memory strengths. If you have a better visual memory, make the information visual in nature. If you have a better verbal memory, make the information verbal in nature. Remember to be creative. You can almost always translate information you need to remember into a form that will work better for you.

WRAPPING IT UP

This chapter is a very basic overview of the way that memory works, and for the most part, we've tailored the information to the needs of this book. As mentioned earlier, in some ways memory can be seen as a metaphor. To talk about memory is to talk about a model of the way the mind works. It is not the thing itself so much as it is a conceptual model of an operating system. There is no single mechanism in your mind that constitutes your memory. Instead, it is a complex array of neurological phenomena that happen throughout the brain.

There are many, many different ways that scientists have thought about memory over time. The processes involved in memory and the differences between verbal and visual memory are nothing more than concepts; they are ways to organize information about the way we think that we use to understand ourselves better.

The concepts in this chapter should help you to make better practical use of your memory, and provide a foundation for the way that we will treat memory in the rest of the book. Our twin goals are to be scientifically accurate and to make this book as usable as possible. To that end, we have tried to keep it simple, but thorough.

In the following chapters we will follow and expand upon this idea and give you more practical ways to improve your memory. But first, in chapter 2, let's figure out exactly what your memory goals are.

2

Getting Started:
Perceptions and Goals

I t is safe to assume your goal in purchasing this book was to improve your memory (unless you simply like collecting books about memory). This assumption suggests that you consider your memory to be faulty. In this chapter, we will discuss your perception of your memory, offer you a brief quiz to evaluate your memory, and help you establish some realistic goals to improve your memory.

YOUR PERCEPTION OF YOUR MEMORY

As the Greek philosopher Epictetus stated, "People are disturbed not by things but by the view which they take of them." Applying this statement to the perception you have of your memory can reveal some interesting information. Do you believe you have a bad memory? Why do you hold this belief? Do you expect your memory to be flawless? Is your ability to recollect slower than it once was? Do you forget the names of acquaintances more frequently now than you did in the past? Nowadays, do you have to write everything down in order to remember it? If you answered yes to these questions, it's safe to assume that you believe you have a "bad" memory.

In today's fast-paced, technological age you may view your memory as a sort of recording device that serves to keep a historical database of your life. You may expect your memory to be perfect, storing and recalling the name of every person you've ever met; tracking all of your appointments, special occasions, and events; detailing project requirements and deadlines; knowing what's in the refrigerator and what ingredients you need to make dinner; and knowing your spouse's, children's, or significant other's schedules and when they will be where. The list of things we expect ourselves to remember is virtually endless. And when we fail to remember even one of these items, we tend to condemn our inability to remember. We tell ourselves that we have a "bad memory" or convince ourselves that we are experiencing the first stages of Alzheimer's disease.

There are some problems with this type of thinking. In the first place, these thoughts are subjective perceptions that you have of your own memory; they are not objective assessments of your actual mental capability. As such, they are immeasurable, not testable, and tend toward negativity. What's more, this negativity creates anxiety and low self-esteem, which will only worsen your memory problems. (Anxiety and other negative emotions adversely affect the ability to remember. See chapter 3 for more information about this.) This kind of negative thinking also makes it impossible for you to develop the necessary skills to improve your memory because it eliminates the possibility for change. The more you convince yourself that you have a "bad memory," the more likely you are to simply accept that as fact and not do the work needed to improve your memory.

To some degree, we are what we think, whether we choose to accept that notion or not. If you believe that you have a "bad memory," you will have one. However, there is a way out of this trap. Before moving on to other aspects of memory, we will first help you work toward a more accepting perception of your memory. We will do this by giving you a short quiz that will help you look at your memory skills more objectively and teach you how to create some concrete memory goals.

Take the following quiz to objectively evaluate how well your memory functions. The Memory Quiz 2000 is reproduced with the kind permission of Gayatri Devi, MD, of the New York Memory and Healthy Aging Services.

MAKING IT WORK:
Test Your Memory

This simple test evaluates some aspects of your memory and cognition. The quiz has two components, a performance section and a historical section.

The Memory Quiz

Part 1

1a. What year is it? _____

1b. What season is it? _____

1c. What month is it? _____

1d. What day of the week is it? _____

1e. What is today's date? _____

2.   Remember these words: apple, table, penny.

3.   Without looking at your watch, write down what time it is: _____ hh:mm

Now look at your watch and write down the actual time: _____ hh:mm

4.   Give the names of the current and previous four U.S. presidents:

_____

_____

_____

_____

5. Give the names of the following items:

a. _____

b. _____

c. _____

d. _____

e. _____

f. _____

g. _____

h. _____

Part 2

Circle the correct answer for each of the following questions:

6. Do you remember the address of the last place you lived?

   Yes   No

7. Do you find that you repeat yourself more often than in the past?

   Yes   No

8. Do people get annoyed with you because of your forgetfulness?

   Yes   No

9. Do you have more trouble remembering lists, such as shopping lists, than in the past?
   Yes   No

10. Do you have trouble remembering events that took place this morning or last week?
    Yes   No

11. Do you now have more trouble following directions than in the past?
    Yes   No

12. Have you been getting lost more often than usual?
    Yes   No

13. Do you have trouble finding the words you need to complete a thought?
    Yes   No

14. Do you find that you lose or misplace things more often than in the past?
    Yes   No

15. Do your memory difficulties impair your work or social life?
    Yes   No

16. Without going back to the beginning of this quiz, write down the three words you were told to remember at the beginning:

_____

_____

_____

SCORING FOR THE MEMORY QUIZ

**Answers for part 1 of the quiz
(total score for part 1 = 18):**

1. Give yourself 1 point for remembering the exact date (date, day of week, month, season, and year). Please note this does not mean giving yourself a point for each of the items; rather give yourself 1 point if all of the date information is correct. (1 point)

2. Did you remember the three words (apple, table, penny) asked for in question 16? Give yourself 1 point for each correct answer. (3 points)

3. If the difference between your guessed time and the correct time is less than thirty minutes, give yourself 1 point. (1 point)

4. Give yourself 1 point for each President named correctly: Bush, Clinton, Bush, Reagan, Carter. The order in which you remembered them is not important. (5 points)

5. Give yourself a point for each correct answer. (8 points)
   a. Abacus (1 point)
   b. Acorn (1 point)
   c. Escalator (1 point)
   d. Igloo (1 point)
   e. Pencil (1 point)
   f. Protractor (1 point)
   g. Pyramid (1 point)
   h. Watch (1 point)

Answers for part 2 of the quiz
(total score for part 2 = 10):

6. Give yourself 1 point for remembering your last address. (1 point)

7–15. Give yourself 1 point each for every question you answered no. (9 points)

Total number of points _____

INTERPRETATION

If you scored a 27 or 28, congratulations! It looks like you have a pretty good memory. This may be a surprising outcome for you, particularly if you bought this book to improve your memory. This should speak to the fact that your perception of your memory may not be an accurate estimate of how well your memory actually operates.

In any event, this book hasn't been a wasted investment. Now, at least you know for sure that you have a pretty decent memory. Nonetheless, even if your test resulted in a very positive finding, working with the strategies in this book can still help you to improve your memory. You did pick up the book for a reason, and we promise to deliver on that.

If you scored between 22 and 26, you're doing all right but you could use some help. This is not to say that you have a "bad memory," just that you could use some help with improving it. You've come to the right place. We are all about helping you 22 to 26ers. If you scored in this range, this book is bound to be of some help to you. Read on, and improve your memory.

If you scored 21 or below, and you've noticed that you're having difficulties with your memory or your thinking abilities of sufficient severity to interfere with your functioning, you probably would benefit from a good neurological evaluation. Don't panic. This test is not a diagnosis. But, if you are having trouble with your memory and you scored in this range, we recommend seeking professional help. You will want to share your concerns with your general practitioner, and you may want to ask that doctor for a referral to a neurologist. A neurologist can give you a battery of various examinations that will help to assess whether you are having cognitive difficulties or not.

SETTING MEMORY GOALS

Now that you have a more objective assessment of how well your memory functions, let's begin establishing some goals to improve your memory in the specific areas where you feel you need help. When setting memory goals, the aim is to achieve realistic improvement of memory functioning. As you create your goals, try to get in touch with those parts of your life that are negatively affected by your memory difficulties.

Be real in assessing where you want to make improvements. If you want to memorize a hundred phone numbers just for the heck of it, we recommend that you buy one of the "memory whiz" programs advertised on TV infomercials. If, however, you are a telephone operator and it will improve the quality of your life to remember a hundred phone numbers, by all means go for it.

The main issue is the quality of your life. How can improving your memory improve your quality of life? What areas do you want to focus on in improving your memory functioning? Are you terrible at remembering names? Appointments? Paying bills on time? Where will improving your memory be likely to help you the most? Once you've figured that out, creating memory goals is a three-step process.

STEP ONE: STATE YOUR GOAL

The first step is simple: State your goal. What do you want to improve? Let's say you never want to forget a name again. Well, say that. If that's your goal, say so. If you want to remember every appointment you make for the rest of your life without a calendar, go ahead and say it. Any goal will do. But remember, if you want this goal to make a difference in your life, it should apply to an area that is giving you sufficient trouble. Don't just pop off a goal to get through this section of the book. Put some effort into it and address something that is really troubling you.

STEP TWO: REDEFINE YOUR GOAL TO MAKE IT ACHIEVABLE

Okay, so you probably aren't going to remember every name or appointment for the rest of your life. That's okay. It doesn't mean you have a faulty memory. It means you're human. To forget is natural. To obsess about forgetting is fruitless. Accept that you will forget sometimes. That way you can make realistic assumptions about your memory rather than putting yourself down every time something slips your mind.

So, now that you have accepted it's okay to experience some forgetfulness, it's time to restate your goal in a realistic fashion. It will be helpful to make this statement as quantitative as possible, so that later you can objectively judge how well you're doing in achieving this goal.

> ## TO FORGET IS NATURAL. TO OBSESS ABOUT FORGETTING IS FRUITLESS.

For example, let's take the goal "I never want to forget another name as long as I live." Well, that's pretty unrealistic. In that amount of time, you might forget your own name. Now reframe the goal so that it is realistically achievable and has quantitatively defined parameters. Something like "I would like to be able to identify 50 percent more of the people in my office by their first and last names." Now this is a goal. It is realistic and has a defined parameter that you can judge objectively later. Use this as a model to define your own memory goals.

STEP THREE: PUT A PLAN OF ACTION INTO YOUR GOAL STATEMENT

In this last step you create an action plan to go along with your goal. Fear not, your action plan doesn't have to be complex. Sometimes, the phrase "action plan" may cause some people to think of a full-fledged military strategy. We do not mean that at all.

ACTION PLANS

An action plan is the exact tactic you intend to use to turn your goal into a reality. At this point, your action plan might be to read this book and incorporate the suggested strategies into your daily life. (At least, this is what we hope your action plan is.) As you progress through the book, you will want to revise your action plan to reflect the results of applying particular strategies taken from the exercises to particular problems with your memory. These could be strategies you take from any chapter. Note that you might want to come back to this part of the goal-creating process once you've read more of the book.

REVISED GOAL WITH ACTION PLAN

For now, let's take a look at your revised goal with this action plan: "I will read this book and incorporate the suggested strategies into my daily life." If you were to include this phrase with your new goal about remembering names, it might look something like this: "I would like to be able to identify 50 percent more of the people in my office by their first and last names. In order to do this, I plan to read *The Memory Doctor* and to use the suggested strategies to make this improvement."

Now you've got something. This is a real, tangible goal with an action plan built into it. You can judge your progress without using the warped lens of your own perceptions about your memory, and you have the means to employ it. This is the kind of process you want to go through for each of your memory goals.

To summarize, the steps in creating your memory goals are as follows:

1. Define your goal.

2. Redefine the goal to make it achievable.

3. Then place an action plan into the goal.

As you establish your goals, state them out loud. How does it make you feel? Anxious? Stressed? As if imminent failure is right around the corner? Then perhaps you are setting your expectations too high and you don't have a clear plan of action. Goals should provide a positive foundation for positive perceptions about yourself and your memory skills. Start out with attainable goals and work up from there.

If the thought of remembering 50 percent more of the names of the people in your office makes you feel anxious, start out with 25 percent more of those names. Once you have achieved this, you can move up to 50 percent. The choices are yours. The main thing is to make your goals realistic and attainable. Otherwise you set yourself up for failure.

REWARD YOUR EFFORTS

It is also important to reward your efforts. Unrewarded goals (just like unrewarded achievements at work) can lead to frustration and a lack of motivation. Document your successes. Figure out what you did to succeed so you can repeat those behaviors. You may even want to keep a memory journal to record your successes. This will give you a tangible record of what you've done and where you've come from (in case you forget).

You may also want to give yourself an actual physical reward for your efforts. When you have achieved your memory goal, treat yourself to dinner out at a good restaurant or a new CD. Do whatever helps you feel good about what you are achieving. This may sound silly, like rewarding a child for doing well in school, but rewarding yourself for your achievements is really worthwhile. The value of behavioral reinforcement of this kind has an enormous body of evidence supporting it. Besides, you deserve the CD or the dinner. This is a great excuse to treat yourself.

More than anything else, try to create lots of positive self-talk for your memory successes. Give yourself some credit for the memory that you have. Your mind, every mind, is a wonder of creation. Honor that. Eliminate negative self-talk for your memory "slips." Think about memory misses in less harsh terms—a memory slip versus a memory failure. Support yourself for the progress you are making. Improving you perception of your memory is akin to improving your self-esteem for your psychological well-being. It is priceless.

PERCEPTIONS OF MEMORY— MISGUIDED GOOD INTENT

"All water has a perfect memory and is forever trying to get back to where it was."

—Toni Morrison (1996)

Let go of the past. We all make the mistake of using our past perceptions about our memories as yardsticks for future expectations of how our memories "should work." We tend to believe that if we continue to test ourselves against our perceptions of how we were in youth, we will "stay young." This won't work for your memory any more than it will work for your waistline. Make the decision right here and now to stop this train of thought.

First of all, since memory is a part of living, and living is a process of learning, your memory is ever changing. Ten years from now, it will not function as it does today. This does not mean it will gradually worsen, only that it will be different. As we add more and more data to our minds, just like the hard drive on a computer, our minds become a little slower. But unlike computers, we become wiser and more accurate with time. Changes in the way memory functions are as natural to aging as the gray hairs that may be creeping into your scalp, or the wrinkles you see around your eyes. It is human, and it is real. That doesn't mean it's bad.

Second, your perceptions about your past memory functions are inaccurate. By definition, when you think that your present memory is bad, using any type of past comparison about how your memory functioned previously will set you up for failure. Besides, if your memory is really as bad as you think it may be, you cannot remember enough detail about your past for an accurate comparison. So stop making the mistake of comparing your memory today to how your memory used to be.

Do this and we promise your memory will improve at least 10 percent right from the start. Before moving on to the next chapter, take some time and outline your personal memory goals. Remember, be specific, make the goals realistic, and put a plan of action into your goal. Once you feel comfortable that your newly established goals are appropriately outlined, let's begin the process of improving your memory with the next chapter, on relaxation.

3

Relax and Remember

Perhaps the following internal monologue will sound
familiar to you:

*I have to be at work early today so that I can prepare
for that meeting with the boss at 9:30 A.M. After that, I
have fifteen calls to make, I have to finish looking over
the report that I'm supposed to turn into the marketing
department, and then I have to . . . oh no! What do I
have to do after that? I know there was something that I
absolutely have to do this afternoon. What is it? Great!
Now I'm really in trouble! Why can't I remember? This
is ridiculous! I'm probably getting early Alzheimer's just*

like my dad did. If that happens, I don't know what I'll
do! What is it that I have to do this afternoon???

And, of course, you don't remember that you were supposed to meet a colleague for lunch until she calls and tells you
that she waited at the restaurant for half an hour before realizing
that you weren't going to show up.

You need to consider reducing the number of tasks you will
try to get done in a day and you should invest in a day-planner.
But if the internal monologue above resonates with you, there is
something else going on. You are stressed out, and stress is affecting your memory.

Nearly all of us have had times when we tried desperately to
remember something and just couldn't. And most of us have
experienced the panic that can follow. It begins when you start to
worry about what might happen if you forget something important. Your worry escalates into panic when you start thinking
that this forgetfulness might be the early onset of Alzheimer's or
that your brain is malfunctioning and you will soon end up in an
amnesiac delirium.

The problem with this kind of thinking (aside from the fact
that the catastrophes you imagine will in all likelihood never happen) is that it affects your ability to remember in a very negative
way. Anxiety inhibits good recall. That's right folks, worrying
about the fact that you can't remember will only compound your
inability to remember. Once you start worrying about remembering, it is unlikely that you will actually be able to do so. Research
has demonstrated that anxiety has a negative impact on memory
(Koltai-Attix, Mason, and Welsh-Bohmer 2003).

HOW ANXIETY AFFECTS YOUR MEMORY

When you become anxious, your mind and body launch into *fight-or-flight* mode. This is a set of psychological and physiological responses that allowed our ancient ancestors to face the terrors of the natural world. Imagine a caveman facing a wooly beast of some sort. The grisly creature bares its teeth, revealing the grue-some remnants of its last meal to your great-great-great-uncle, who is about to become its next meal. This guy better get ready to run like mad or fight like hell.

Luckily, the caveman's body and mind were programmed to do just that. As he looked into that awful maw, his blood pressure went up, sending more oxygen throughout his body and to his brain allowing him to run faster, move more quickly, and see more clearly. However, the last thing your endangered relative needed to think about was what he had for dinner the night before or when his kids were due home from hunting lessons.

To keep his mind focused on the immediate necessity of staying alive, the higher-level neurological functions of his brain actually shut down to a degree. This included his memory. Studies have shown that the oxygen intake to the parts of the brain that control higher cognitive functioning—like mem-ory—is shunted elsewhere in the brain. This allows the regions of the brain that ensure survival more "brainpower" (Mason 2003).

Fortunate or unfortunate as it may be, our physiological evolution has not kept up with the pace of our rapidly changing society. It is unlikely that many of us will ever look into the

> **ANXIETY LITERALLY PROHIBITS MEMORY.**
> **THE ANTIDOTE TO ANXIETY IS RELAXATION.**

hungry mouth of a creature wanting to eat us. But our bodies and minds are programmed to respond to stressful situations as though we were doing just that. That holds true for the kind of catastrophic thinking that goes on when you become worried about not being able to remember and what the possible reasons for not remembering could be.

If you have thoughts like "I must be getting Alzheimer's" or "If I don't remember what I need to right now, the consequences will be horrible," you are making yourself anxious and setting off the autonomic nervous system responses that lead to the fight-or-flight mode. Anxiety literally prohibits memory. The antidote to anxiety is relaxation. So let's explore what that means a bit, and then we'll give you some exercises that will help you to relax.

WHAT DOES IT MEAN TO RELAX?

Anxiety cannot exist in a relaxed body. These two states of being are antithetical. And, as you know, anxiety prohibits good memory. What this all boils down to is that there is hope. If you can manage to relax, you will decrease your anxiety and thereby improve your memory. The problem is that many of us have never really experienced true relaxation, and even if we have, how can we get into that relaxed frame of mind when we are busy working, taking care of the kids, and trying to spend some quality time with our partner? Well, we have some answers for you.

Relaxation is a physiological state just as anxiety is. It is marked by reduced heart rate, reduced respiration rate, and reduced oxygen consumption. In essence, it is exactly the opposite of anxiety. When your body is using up less oxygen for fight-or-flight mode, that means more oxygen is available for use in the other parts of your brain, including the parts responsible for memory.

When you deeply relax, your body and mind slow down and you feel quiet and peaceful. In our busy society, we are no longer accustomed to getting into this state, and thus it has to be cultivated. Sitting down to watch TV or taking a coffee break so you can run across the street to buy junk food at the corner store will not get you into a deeply relaxed state. It won't even get you into a lightly relaxed state. It may even stress you out further. If you are as busy as most of us are, you will need to learn how to relax properly.

Most of the leading books on anxiety suggest that you institute a "relaxation program" into your daily schedule. This amounts to spending between half an hour and an hour every day practicing relaxation techniques like progressive muscle relaxation, abdominal breathing, meditation, or visualization. If you can manage this, that's great. There is no doubt that learning to relax at this level will help you when you are searching to recover a lost or forgotten memory.

But this type of regimen is not required for you to relax enough to improve your memory. Instead, we will teach you a few techniques that you can employ quickly, in the exact moment when you forget something. You will then be able to relax your mind and body enough so that your upper-level cognitive functions can receive the needed energy for you to find the information you are looking for.

RELAXATION FOR RECALL

So, there you are sitting in your chair at the office, and you know you've forgotten what you are supposed to do at 10:30 A.M. today. You're certain you had something scheduled, but you forgot to write it down in your day-planner and now you can't remember it. You start to get angry with yourself and say, "Oh great! Why do I always do this?" You stare at your computer monitor, and if looks could kill, the computer would explode. You start clenching your teeth and your shoulders tighten. You say, "This is just ridiculous. I can't stand it when I can't remember," again and again to yourself.

At this point, the best thing you can do to remember what you need to remember is to take a break, just for a few minutes, to use one of the following exercises. Not only will doing an exercise restrain your desire to pick up your office chair and smash your computer with it (a strategy that will get you nowhere), it will actually improve your ability to recall.

ABDOMINAL BREATHING

Most people don't even know what it means to take a full breath. Breathing well is a lost art in modern society, particularly in Western cultures. Many cultures in the East have expanded breathing techniques into both rituals and practices. Because breathing is controlled by the autonomic nervous system, which means it occurs involuntarily, we tend to ignore the importance of breath. But here's the thing: If you don't breathe, you will die. This is a truth that we all understand. What's more, breathing well has enormous health benefits, both physically and psychologically. You may have noticed that these days most "complete health programs" have a breathing component to them.

For your purposes it is important to recognize that breathing deeply will reduce your anxiety, increase your sense of relaxation, and thus improve your ability to recall. It also has the benefit of oxygenating your blood more completely. This oxygen-rich blood will flow through the parts of your brain that govern memory, thus supplying more "power" to those parts. So let's put breathing well into practice. The following exercise will teach you how to breathe deeply.

MAKING IT WORK:
Abdominal Breathing

The first thing you will want to do in this exercise is get yourself into a comfortable position. What this position is depends on where you are. If you are in your office, you may want to close the door (if you have one), lean back in your chair, put your feet up on the desk, and unbutton the top button of your pants (don't forget to rebutton it when the exercise is finished). If you are at home, you may want to lie down in your bed or relax in a recliner. Make your choices based on accessibility and the realities of your situation. A place to practice doesn't have to be elaborate or complicated, and it doesn't have to be a big hassle. If you can't manage to find a completely relaxed position, simply doing this exercise while standing in place with your eyes closed will be helpful.

Once you've made yourself comfortable, place one of your hands on your stomach and the other hand on your chest. Close your eyes so you can concentrate completely on your breathing. Feel your breath come in and go out. Notice which part of your body expands as you inhale. Is it your chest or your belly? If you are like most of us, your chest will expand as you inhale. You want to change this. Make an effort to breathe into the bottom of your lungs. You will know this is happening when you feel your stomach expand while your chest remains relatively flat. Once you have achieved this, do the following cycle for five repetitions: Inhale to the count of five, then exhale to the count of five. As you do this, you may want to repeat the word "relax" to yourself.

Don't rush. Make sure that you are slowly counting to five on both the inhale and the exhale.

Inhale . . . 2 . . . 3 . . . 4 . . . 5

Exhale . . . 2 . . . 3 . . . 4 . . . 5

Try to inhale completely, making your stomach a bit round, but not taut. Do the same on the exhale. Expel as much oxygen from your lungs as you can without causing yourself to hyperventilate. Breathe slowly and completely. Take your time. If you find that a count of five doesn't work for you, you may want to increase it to a count of ten. Do what works for you.

This exercise should take between one and two minutes to complete. Once you have done your repetitions, also called "reps," check yourself out. Do you feel more relaxed?

TENSE AND RELAX: A SHORT FORM OF PROGRESSIVE MUSCLE RELAXATION

You may have heard of progressive muscle relaxation (PMR). This is a systematic way of tensing and relaxing all of the major muscle groups in the body. The system was developed by Edmund Jacobsen over fifty years ago (1974). Dr. Jacobsen found that by intentionally tensing and relaxing muscle groups in the body, people could learn how to release tension that they didn't even know they had in these muscle groups. For more than half a century, this technique has demonstrated immense health benefits.

To do a complete PMR cycle takes about half an hour. Clearly, there is no way you will have the time to do this when you are busy managing your life and are trying to remember something on the go. Instead, what we would like to teach you is a dramatically shortened way to tense and relax certain muscle groups in your body in order to generate a relaxation response that will help improve your recall.

MAKING IT WORK: Tense and Relax

To do this exercise most effectively it's a good idea to get yourself into a comfortable position, much as you did for the "Abdominal Breathing" exercise above. Once you have done this, follow the guidelines below.

It's also a good idea to go through the entire regimen systematically, in the order given, if you can manage that. By doing this, you will relax all of the major muscle groups in your body, and this will be very helpful to your memory. If this is not possible (for example, you might have shoes on that won't allow you to do the feet exercise), or if you feel that you just don't have the time, don't worry about it. You can shorten the exercise by just relaxing the muscle groups that are the easiest for you to do on the spot.

We do, however, recommend that you do some of the exercises that will affect a large group of muscles. That way, it will be much easier to feel the relaxation response. If you just clench and release your fists, it is unlikely that you will feel a big difference, but if you do the same with your stomach muscles or the large muscles in your legs, you will get a much better response.

Do each of the following tense-and-relax cycles for ten to fifteen seconds. Hold the tension to the count of fifteen and then relax to the count of fifteen. As you relax, try to feel all of the tension flowing away and relaxation settling in deeper and deeper in these muscle groups.

FEET AND CALVES

Tense: Extend your legs at the knee and point your toes straight out in front of you. Curl your toes downward so that you scrunch up your foot into a kind of fist.

Relax: Bring your feet and legs back to a relaxed and settled position.

THIGHS AND BUTTOCKS

Tense: Again, extend your leg at the knee. This time, relax your foot and press your leg down as much as possible so that your thigh is doing most of the work. At the same time, squeeze your buttocks together. If you are sitting in a chair, you should feel yourself rise up a little as you squeeze your buttocks.

Relax: Bring your feet and legs back to a relaxed position, and relax your buttocks so that you are sitting flat on your chair again.

BACK

Tense: Arch your back, shoulders, and neck so that you can feel all the muscles along your spine.

Relax: Resume your previous position. You can even slump a little to reverse the arch of your back so that you relax your muscles more fully.

STOMACH

Tense: Act as though you are doing a "mini-sit-up" by clenching the muscles in your abdomen.

Relax: Let go of the "mini-sit-up" pose. You may even want to push out your stomach just a little to increase the effect.

(Note that this is an extremely effective exercise that you can do anywhere. If done properly, it is hardly noticeable and can be performed in a supermarket or at a business meeting. It is also extremely effective due to the fact that your abdominal muscles are some of the biggest muscles in your body.)

SHOULDERS

Tense: Raise your shoulders up toward your ears.

Relax: Let go of the pose and allow your arms to dangle freely at your sides.

ARMS

Tense: Hold your arms straight out in front of you at shoulder height. Clench your fists, and tighten your biceps and triceps.

Relax: Again, allow your arms to hang down freely at your sides.

JAW, NECK, AND FACE

Tense: Clench your teeth, frown, and furrow your brow.

Relax: Let the tension go. Let your jaw hang down a little bit. Feel the muscles in your forehead smooth out.

SLUMPING

Have you ever come home after a long, hard day and thrown yourself down in a chair or on the sofa and just lain there like a Raggedy Ann doll? It feels great doesn't it? It's so relaxed, you could almost fall asleep just thinking about it. This is a technique that we fondly refer to as "slumping," and it is a great way to relax.

MAKING IT WORK: Slumping

This one is really simple. Sit down on a bed or a chair, again, wherever is convenient based on your surroundings, and just let all of the tension flow out of your body. Think of yourself as a floppy doll. Clear your mind and just slump. Let the tension go out of your shoulders, let your arms hang at your sides, let your head hang down onto your chest, and let your jaw drop open. If you need to, stick your legs out in front of you. Do whatever you can to make yourself floppy.

It's important that you don't slump and try to remember at the same time. Allow your mind to be as blank as your body is. Remember, a Raggedy Ann doll can't think anymore than she can move. Be that doll. If you are really wound up, you may want to take a few abdominal breaths before you start doing the slumping exercise.

Once you have slumped for a minute or two, bring yourself back to your human self. Sit up in your chair and resume whatever it was you were doing, namely using that memory of yours.

VISUALIZATION

Visualization is a *mental exercise*. All the other techniques in this chapter have a very strong physical component. This does not. One reason for this is that many people find it easier to feel an immediate sense of relaxation when they are able to ground themselves in their physical reality. Nonetheless, visualization is a very powerful relaxation tool when used effectively.

Like abdominal breathing and PMR, visualization can be a very complex exercise. Entire books have been published about the subject. If you decide to, you can turn visualization into a regular daily practice. At its most sophisticated, it becomes a form of self-hypnosis. It can take a lot of time and a lot of energy to do it on this scale. And, like many of the other exercises presented in this chapter, visualization has been proven to have extraordinary psychological and physical health benefits. It is truly a wonder what the mind can do.

Many of the available visualization exercises have predescribed programs for inducing a semihypnotic state, and they take you on an actual mental journey that has been prepared in advance. There are many tapes on the market that will guide you on a visualization trip through a beautiful forest, along white sand beaches where the ocean roars, or across a lovely bridge spanning a babbling brook. These are wonderful exercises, but they are time-consuming. We will ask you to do something a little different. We suggest that you make up your own visualization.

MAKING IT WORK: Visualization

Everyone has certain times in the day when they slip off into daydreams. What we suggest here is that you put those times to work for you as a way to relax.

Get into that comfortable position again, close your eyes, and let your mind drift. Doing a bit of abdominal breathing in advance can help prepare you for this exercise, so give that a try if you like.

As your mind starts to wander, bring something into the darkness that gives you pleasure and makes you feel at peace.

This might be a favorite vacation you've taken or a childhood memory. It could be a passage in a favorite novel or a painting you love. If you are creative, it might be an entirely new scene that you make up on the spot. Try to make your imagination work for you. Imagine the sights and sounds in detail. Can you smell the flowers there on the side of the cobblestone road? Can you see the beautiful colors of the tropical fish in that aquarium you've always wanted?

Now, put yourself into the scene. See yourself walking down a quiet cobblestone road in a small village hundreds of years ago. There on the corner is your favorite pub. It's dark and the smell of bread and beer and sausage wafts through the door. You step in. What happens next is up to you. This is your visualization. This is your time to relax.

Once you feel relaxed and the scene has played itself out in your mind, slowly bring yourself back to your surroundings. You may want to stay seated for a few minutes and readjust to your setting before going back to real life.

TIP: After completing any of the exercises above, gently bring what you were trying to remember back to your consciousness. If you rush back to remembering right after finishing the exercise, you will undo all the good you've accomplished with the relaxation. Start looking for the information in your mind again. But do it slowly. It is there. Relax and it will come to you.

PUTTING IT ALL TOGETHER

That's it! Now you know how to relax. Well, maybe not quite. True relaxation takes practice. But if you put these exercises to work for you and you use them when you need them, soon enough you'll learn to relax deeply, and by doing so, you will improve your memory.

One of the great things about the exercises we have given you in this chapter is that you can use them in tandem. That is, you can do more than one exercise at a time. You might have noticed that we suggested starting with a little abdominal breathing before some of the exercises above. That is only one possible combination. You can slump and visualize, you can do abdominal breathing while practicing the tense-and-relax cycles. It's all up to you.

TIP: Another way to improve your memory is to use relaxation while encoding. Do you remember from chapter 1 that encoding is defined as the process that takes place when you put information into your brain? If you are tense, you won't be able to encode well. This means that your recall will subsequently be that much more difficult. To improve your memory, do any of the relaxation exercises from this chapter before you encode important information. A few abdominal breaths will serve you well in this capacity.

The more effectively you learn to relax in the moment, the more effectively you will be able to remember. Your memory will improve dramatically as your ability to relax improves.

Now that you are nice and relaxed, chapter 4 will teach you to sit up and pay attention. Remember to take your new relaxation skills with you throughout your reading of this book. They will help you in more ways than you can imagine.

4

Pay Attention!

"Pay attention!" While you were growing up, you probably heard this phrase at least several hundred times from parents, teachers, aunts, uncles, you name it. You may still hear it from your spouse or partner if you are in the habit of watching TV or reading the paper while he or she is talking. But what does this phrase really mean and what is the value of "paying attention"?

In our lives we are expected to know almost instinctively what "paying attention" means. To pay attention is a cognitive function, like memory, that works so naturally we don't even think about it most of the time. Nonetheless, all too often we don't pay attention.

> ## BETTER ATTENTION EQUALS BETTER MEMORY.

The truth of the matter is that paying attention is a very sophisticated cognitive process that serves as the foundation for virtually all other cognitive functions. You use attention when you look at something, when you listen to something, when you speak, even when you eat. And attention is especially important to memory. The basic rule is this: The more attention you pay to a set of data, the more likely you are to remember that data. Better attention equals better memory. This being the case, paying attention to attention is a very important step toward improving your memory.

So to go back to the question at hand: What is attention? One of the definitions that *Merriam-Webster's Collegiate Dictionary* (11th edition) provides says that attention is "the act or state of attending especially through applying the mind to an object of sense or thought." This is pretty good as far as it goes, but understanding what attention is and how it functions in your brain to help you improve your memory will take a bit more of an explanation.

PASSIVE VS. ACTIVE ATTENTION

We must interrupt this chapter to ask you an important memory question. Do you remember the name of the person who wrote the second endorsement on the back cover of this book? Probably not. Go ahead and turn to the back cover now, and commit that name to memory. Pay attention to the name. We promise this will pay off.

Now back to our regularly scheduled program . . .

Attention is, essentially, your ability to focus on something. Normally this is done for a specific purpose. But there are many different types of attention that you can pay to any given activity. However, before discussing the different types of attention, let's start with some more basic attributes of attention.

You can engage in anything that you do either actively or passively. If you are actively engaged in something, that means you are consciously aware of what you are doing and you are putting some effort into it. When you are passively engaged, you are less conscious of what you're doing and you're not really that invested in the event.

For example, let's say that your car has broken down and you need to get to the bus stop so you can meet a friend for lunch. You're annoyed that you can't drive, but it isn't the end of the world. Now, you can take this walk in one of two ways. You can actively engage in the walk, enjoying the cool air, looking at the sights around you, and consciously feeling the sun on your face. You may even decide to use the opportunity to get a little exercise and turn it into a power walk. On the other hand, you could passively walk to the bus stop, letting your body follow the route automatically, and just kind of space out until you board the bus.

The same choices are true of attention. You can either actively pay attention to something or you can passively pay attention to it. In the example above, you were going to get to the bus stop either way, so the consequences of being passive were minimal. However, when it comes to memory, the difference between actively paying attention and passively paying attention is huge. There is one main reason for this: The more actively you pay attention, the better you will be able to encode information into your memory. Wait! What does "encoding" mean? If you remember, good for you. If you don't, no worries; go back to chapter 1 and refresh your memory.

As you know from chapter 1, the single most valuable change you can make to create a difference in the way your memory works will be during your encoding process. (See chapter 5 for suggestions on improving your encoding process.) The more actively you pay attention to a set of data when you first encounter it, the stronger the neural networks related to this data will become. Stronger neural networks mean easier recall, which means good memory. The point of this discussion is just a more elaborate repetition of what you heard all those years while you were growing up: "Pay attention!"

MAKING IT WORK:
Passive vs. Active Attention

Earlier we asked you to commit to memory a name from the back cover. Did you do it? If not, shame on you. If you did, write the name below (or, if you hate writing in your books, you can just call it to mind).

Now check the name you wrote or recalled against the back cover. Is it the right name? Good job. You did it. You passed the test.

You may be wondering now whether the authors have temporarily lost their minds. Rest assured. They are fine. Or perhaps you've have seen through our little ruse. Ah yes, this little test was done for a greater purpose.

The idea behind this exercise was to give you some direct experience with the difference between active and passive attention. When we first asked you to recall the name earlier in this chapter you probably were not able to do it. If you were able to do it, either you don't need this book or you have an obsession with endorsements. In all likelihood, you glanced at the back cover of the book when you bought it, you may even have read the name and the endorsement, but you probably didn't put too much effort into actively remembering it. That is, you paid passive attention to the name.

When we asked you to recall the name the second time, however, it is very likely that you were able to do just that. That's because you went to the back cover, looked at the name, actively paid attention to it, and thus encoded it in your memory. If this worked out the way we planned it to, that is proof of the important difference between active and passive attention. Moreover, it proves our contention that active attention does, in fact, improve memory.

We now give you permission to purge that name from your memory for all time.

Thank you for participating. This has been a test of the emergency memory system.

If you want an easy way to improve your memory, take this concept with you beyond the pages of this book and start to pay active attention to the things you want to remember. If you really need to remember to pick up Tommy from soccer practice so that he won't have to walk home uphill in the snow, then actively pay attention when he tells you what time practice will be over. Being actively engaged at the moment of encoding is probably the best thing you can do for your memory.

TYPES OF ATTENTION

It's fairly easy to note the difference between active and passive attention. However, the process of paying attention is actually more complex than just those two divisions. In 1988, Lazar Stankov identified six different types of attention. What follows is a brief review of these different types:

Concentration is the ability to sustain directed mental energy for a particular task for an extended period of time. Think of reading a book that is a little beyond your normal reading comprehension level. This requires concentration.

Vigilance is the ability to detect rarely occurring symbols over an extended period of time. Watching for falling stars is a good example of being vigilant.

Search is your ability to pick out a particular type of data among other similar data. Being able to pick out a specific name from a list of names in the telephone directory is an example of search. The word searches you find in puzzle books or "Where's Waldo" puzzles are also examples of search.

Selective attention is the ability to direct your mental energy toward one activity while blocking out other information that may be competing for your attention. Reading a book while your spouse is on the phone is an example of selective attention.

(Remember, this is different than "selective listening," a skill that will surely destroy your relationship.)

Alternating attention is the ability to switch back and forth between attending to two different stimuli. Reading a book and watching the news is an example of alternating attention.

Divided attention is the ability to perform two different tasks at the same time. Listening to music while washing the dishes is a good example of divided attention.

But what does all his mean for you? Why should you care if there are six different types of attention? After all, you are not a neuropsychologist (unless you are, in which case we apologize). There are two reasons that you should care. In the first place, choosing the type of attention that you use for a given activity has been shown to improve memory (Niemann, Ruff, and Baser 1990).

In the second place, the higher-order types of attention—selective attention, alternating attention, and divided attention—actually take a fair amount of cognitive energy. Being

TIP! Working with puzzle books is one way to improve your attention skills. Word searches, mazes, and crossword puzzles exercise many of the same skills that are required to pay good attention. So, one simple and fun way to improve your attention and your memory would be to spend a little time working with puzzle books.

> **GOOD EFFORT IS RESPECTFUL OF LIMITS.**

conscious of the type of attention you are using will allow you to focus your cognitive energy where you want it more effectively. This, in effect, will improve your memory.

But what do we mean by "cognitive energy," and how does that affect memory?

COGNITIVE ENERGY AND FATIGUE

Up to this point you may have gotten the impression that what we want you to do is to put more effort into the way that you pay attention. That's exactly right. Attention takes effort, and effort is what will improve your memory. But here's the tricky part: Good effort is respectful of limits.

Each of us has only a finite amount of cognitive energy (some of us more finite than others). These limited resources must be used carefully because overdoing it just makes matters worse. The area that you want to be conscious of is where you put your energy.

We could teach you how to remember a hundred names from a very large group of people the way memory experts do on TV with their studio audiences, but what is the value of that? What would it really get you? Even the exercise above, when we asked you to remember a name from the back cover of this book, borders on being valueless (luckily, we were able to save it from that fate).

The point is this: You cannot remember everything, nor would you want to. If you spent your life being actively attentive all the time and tried to remember every detail from every day's events, you would become exhausted very quickly, and then you would go mad. Our brains naturally default into passivity as a way of storing our cognitive energy for what is really important.

You know where you are having problems with your memory (chapter 2 should have helped you with that) and you know what you want to remember better. The idea is to apply the exercises and concepts throughout this book to those areas, not to all areas.

When you are mentally fatigued, your cognitive energy resources are depleted. If you try too hard, you will actually inhibit your ability to remember. Certain types of attention require an immense amount of cognitive energy, particularly selective attention, alternating attention, and divided attention. You may notice that when you try to read a book and watch the news at the same time, you don't remember either very well. In part, this is due to the fact that you are using your limited cognitive resources quite poorly. Each of those activities requires a lot of attention. If you divide what you have between them, it is quite likely that you won't remember either of them very well.

One of the major reasons that people in our culture are having memory problems is that there is too much going on. We just can't process it all. It would be nice if we could, but that isn't the reality. So be good to yourself and be good to your memory. Respect your limits. You will find that you will actually remember far more if you allow yourself not to remember everything.

WETT

WETT is an acronym for a method of conserving energy cognitive energy. It comes from the first letters of these four phrases:

- Write it down

- Eliminate distractions

- Take breaks

- Timing

The acronym will help you to remember the method more easily. Follow these steps, and you'll be able to save your cognitive resources for really important matters.

WRITE IT DOWN

One of the best strategies you can use to conserve your cognitive resources is to take notes or keep an appointment calendar. Keep in mind that notes in and of themselves do not create a better memory. Notes must be used within the context of organization; that is to say, lost notes won't do anyone any good. Place notes strategically throughout your environment. If you must make a phone call first thing in the morning, place a note next to your toothbrush. If you need to remember to stop at the post office on the way home from work, place a note on the dashboard of your car. By keeping notes you won't have to focus on trying to remember every detail of your day, reserving what memory you have for matters that are really important.

ELIMINATE DISTRACTIONS

The thing that is so annoying about listening to your spouse talking on the phone while you're trying to read a book is that you can't concentrate on your book. That is, you've been forced into using selective attention rather than concentration. As mentioned above, selective attention, in general, uses a lot more of your cognitive resources than concentration does.

The solution to this problem is to eliminate the distraction. Mind you, this does not mean eliminating your spouse. Rather, you can simply move into another room where you can't hear the telephone conversation and thus can more easily concentrate on your book.

If there is something really important you need to remember, even before paying attention to it, eliminate everything in your environment that might distract you. Sometimes this may take a little while to figure out. In a lot of cases, this will mean that you've given yourself the opportunity to move from a higher-order type of attention, such as selective attention, to a lower-order type of attention, such as concentration. This can be very helpful.

Ironically, while I was writing this, I started noticing that I was having a hard time concentrating. It took me a few minutes to realize the music I was listening to was distracting me. I couldn't pay attention to my writing because my cognitive resources were preoccupied by listening to the group Dead Can Dance.

TAKE BREAKS

If you're at work and you need to memorize some sales figures for the afternoon meeting, the best way to begin is to take a little break before you look at the figures.

Lots of times we get so busy that we don't even realize we are using up our cognitive energy. Virtually everything that we do uses some cognitive energy. (Sleeping is the only activity I can think of that doesn't require cognitive energy, and you have no hope of trying to remember anything while you are asleep anyway).

If you find you are having trouble remembering, make sure you are well rested and that you don't have a whole lot of other stuff on your mind when you try to remember something. A short break is far more valuable than forcing yourself to concentrate when you are already tired.

TIP: When you take a break, it's a good idea to do some of the relaxation exercises described in chapter 3. This will have the dual benefit of reducing your cognitive exhaustion and improving your memory by reducing stress and anxiety. Breaks and relaxation exercises are a very powerful, winning combination.

TIMING

There are times when you know you will be distracted and unable to concentrate. Don't try to remember too much during those times. For example, if you've decided that you want to memorize Hamlet's third soliloquy because you missed out on that opportunity in high school, trying to do that when the kids come home after school is probably not the best time. Wait until you can get some quiet space, then work on the memorization.

In some cases, you won't be able to choose the circumstances when you have to remember something. However, you will find that in many situations you actually have more control over this issue than you think you have.

PUTTING IT ALL TOGETHER

If you want to make the most of your memory, you will take all of the suggestions in this chapter and apply them to your life in ways that make sense to you. All this information about attention is so intimately related that, in some ways, the divisions drawn between the types of attention used are arbitrary intellectual constructs built only to help you understand attention and the role it plays in memory a little better.

The main point to take away from this chapter is that you need to pay attention in order to remember, and the more conscious you are of this, the better you will be able to remember.

That is the bottom line. Get conscious about attention. Think about what may be distracting you. Think about the type of attention you use for any given task. Be active rather than passive when you encounter new information.

Once you learn to pay attention to attention you will begin to understand what having a "good memory" feels like.

5

Putting Information In and Getting It Back Out

As the title indicates, this chapter is all about putting information into your brain (encoding) and getting it back out again (retrieval). You may have noticed that we tend to focus a whole lot more on encoding than we do on retrieval. You may even have said to yourself, "But that isn't my problem! I can put information into my brain just fine. My problem is memory! I just can't seem to get the information back out once it has gone in there." You may be worried that this book isn't about memory at all. You may be carrying a chicken under your arm while reading this book.

Your brain is not some vacuous black hole that information gets sucked into never to be seen again. Or, at least for the purposes of this book, we will assume that your brain is not a vacuous black hole. If it is, your problems are well beyond the scope of our work here.

Most of us tend to focus so heavily on the retrieval part of the memory system that we don't even give much attention to the encoding part of the memory process. We assume that if our brain were okay, it would do its job the way it's supposed to and we would automatically encode the information we need to remember without any effort. When recall doesn't come as quickly as we would like it to, we tend to make excuses, think disparaging thoughts about ourselves, or believe that we are broken in some way. We tell ourselves, "I guess I'm just getting old. The old brain doesn't work the way it used to," or "I'm so stupid. I can't remember anything."

These patterns of thought are fallacious. The truth of the matter is that you wouldn't have a problem retrieving information if it had been properly encoded in the first place. The better the encoding, the stronger the neural networks that contain the memory. If you haven't created sufficiently strong neural networks, it is very unlikely that you will be able to retrieve any memory with ease. So, instead of worrying so much about getting information back out of your memory, you should focus on putting good information into your brain. Encoding is the keystone to a good memory.

**ENCODING IS THE KEYSTONE
TO A GOOD MEMORY.**

That being said, most of this chapter will focus on encoding strategies. These are vastly more important than retrieval strategies. There are, however, some ways that you can improve your retrieval as well, and we will also give you some ways to do that.

ENCODING

In chapter 4 you learned about attention and the importance of paying attention for developing a more powerful memory. It is true that attention is extremely important. However, encoding requires more than paying attention. Encoding is all about using your higher cognitive functions (yes, you do have these) to elaborate and deepen the neural networks that contain memories. For example, you could pay active attention to a phone number by eliminating the distractions around you and then stare at the number written on a piece of paper. You may be able to remember the number by doing this. However, there are several more effective ways to encode this same phone number more deeply into your memory. The first of these is rehearsal.

REHEARSAL

Rehearsal is the act of repeating something over and over again until it is etched in your brain. It is one of the most natural and most efficient ways to improve your encoding. If you were trying to memorize a phone number, it's likely that you would say the number aloud to yourself over and over again until you were confident that you "had it." This is rehearsal.

Right now, think of a piece of information that you will never forget. Take your spouse's name for example. How many times have you rehearsed that name? How many times have you said that name aloud or in your head? Millions? Billions? The many times you said the name strengthened the neural networks related to the name to such an extent that the name can never be forgotten. That's the value of rehearsal.

But remember that rehearsal (or for that matter any encoding strategy) does not work independent of attention. You want to use your attention skills at the same time you use your encoding skills. If you were to halfheartedly say the phone number you want to remember over and over again without putting much cognitive effort, that is, attention, into it, it's not likely you will remember it for very long. If, on the other hand, you think about your surroundings, choose the type of attention you intend to employ, use some of the WETT skills that you learned in chapter 4, and *then* start to rehearse, you will maximize your chances of remembering the information exponentially (that means a lot).

TIP: Another technique you might want to try is to rehearse in cycles. Rather than sitting down and spending half an hour trying to remember a phone number, do it in two to five-minute intervals. In this way, you will conserve cognitive energy and give yourself a built-in "test" of the information. This can be much more powerful than spending large amounts of time trying to encode.

ELABORATION

Let's say that you are getting ready to go to the grocery store, and on your way out of the house, your significant other yells, "Honey, could you remember to pick up some cream cheese and some stewed tomatoes? I really like the Del Monte stewed tomatoes, so if they have those, get them." You, of course, have already prepared your list of grocery items in your head, carefully using memory strategies from this book to make sure that you don't forget anything. Now, at the last minute, you have to plug something new into that list. What to do?

Using elaboration is another powerful way to improve your encoding process. *Elaboration* is the act of expanding the immediate context of the information you want to remember so that it includes more sensory or cognitive components. When you want to remember something, the value of including more parts of your brain in the encoding process is that it gives you that many more neural traces to use later when you want to retrieve the memory.

There is a large body of evidence indicating that when we include more of our cognitive structures in the creation of a memory, that memory will be embedded more deeply in the brain (Yesavage 1989). There are a number of different ways that you can elaborate on the information you want to remember, and once you learn to be creative with elaboration, it can be quite a lot of fun. Let's go through a few examples.

GET YOUR SENSES INVOLVED

Perhaps the most direct way to elaborate on the information you need to remember is to get your senses involved with the information. When we are trying to remember, we tend to get stuck in the verbal component of the information. For example, you could use your rehearsal strategies and say, "cream cheese and Del Monte stewed tomatoes" over and over again to yourself. This may serve you fairly well. But remember that words are only descriptors. They stand for real things (at least a whole lot of them do). It can be helpful to move beyond the words and go back to the thing at hand.

That means you want to deconstruct the word so that you get back to the physical and sensory properties of the object the word describes. Think about cream cheese. It's a white, creamy substance that you spread on your bagels. Think about the consistency of it. Think about how it tastes. In fact, you can visualize it (see the section "Visualization" below) and bring the cream cheese into your mind's eye. Think about how cream cheese would feel if you were to smear it between your hands. Now do the same with stewed tomatoes. Imagine squishing slimy slices of tomatoes, canned for future use, in your hands. Imagine them in the stew your spouse will make with them for dinner that night. You can take this process as far as your imagination will let you.

MAKE UP A STORY

There is one problem you might confront when using elaborate sensory information. Some information does not relate to the senses. In the example above, you were asked to pick up some *Del Monte* stewed tomatoes. These aren't just any old stewed tomatoes. These are a special brand of stewed tomatoes. What kind of sensory information can you attribute to Del Monte? We'll give you a hint—none.

For this reason, in certain circumstances it can be useful to use other types of elaboration techniques. One of these is to make up a story about the things you want to remember. This may sound a little silly, but it can be really fun (as long as you allow yourself to be creative with it), and it's amazing how effective this method can be for helping your memory. There are three things you will want to remember when creating your story.

1. **Use all of the elements you need to remember in your story.** In the example above, there are two things that you need to remember: cream cheese and Del Monte stewed tomatoes. This may sound too simplistic, but you will want to make sure these items are in the story you create.

2. **Use humor.** We tend to remember things that make us laugh or are non sequiturs much better than we remember things that are meaningless. Thus, using humor can be really helpful for improving your memory. Remember the comment about carrying a chicken under your arm above? That's the kind of thing that is bound to stand out in a story and make you remember it. No, we don't really believe that you are carrying a chicken under your arm while reading this book.

3. **Use your other encoding strategies.** All of these techniques can be used interdependently. It's great if you can use more than one strategy at a time. In your story you might want to rehearse by making sure that you say the names of the things you need to remember over and over again, or you might want to use a lot of sensory information. If you use both of these, that will surely enhance your memory.

Now we will give you an example of the kind of story you might create about cream cheese and Del Monte stewed tomatoes. This will be a bit of levity after all the hard work you have done up to this point.

THE SECRET OF DEL MONTE STEWED TOMATOES: CREAM CHEESE

Del Monte was a small man, not more than three feet tall. He had ruddy cheeks, a square, stocky frame, and was covered in hair from head to foot. He drank bourbon like a fish. Del Monte was famous throughout the land for making the most delicious stewed tomatoes. No one knew what his secret was, they only knew that once you had eaten a can of Del Monte stewed tomatoes you would never try any other.

Many years ago Del Monte discovered the secret of great stewed tomatoes: cream cheese. One day, after having one too many swigs from his bourbon flask, Del Monte decided that to add a tablespoon of cream cheese to his next batch of stewed tomatoes. Little did he know what a treat it would turn out to be.

He spooned out a tablespoon of the white, creamy stuff from its container and dumped it into the vat in which he was cooking his stewed tomatoes. The cheese slowly dissolved into the red soup of the stewed tomatoes. After he tasted his new creation, he knew he had found the recipe for perfect stewed tomatoes: cream cheese.

As you can see, your story need not have any basis in reality. In fact, in some cases the more bizarre the story is, the easier you will be able to remember the essential components. Just have fun with it, be creative, and enjoy remembering.

VISUALIZATION

The last encoding strategy we would like to teach you about in this chapter is visualization. Chapter 3 has some information about visualization, as well. But for the purposes of this book, we separated the visualization exercises according to their direct applications to memory. You may want to refer to chapter 3, however, for a little more information about this technique.

In recent years, visualization has become a kind of practice, or discipline, on its own. It is well-known that visualization can have a major impact on everything from your physical and psychological health to your ability to learn (and relax . . . remember?). Indeed visualization can be invaluable in developing a good memory.

Currently, there are a number of books on visualization on the market, and if you are really attracted to this technique you might consider buying one. We recommend *Visualization for Change* (1994) by Patrick Fanning, published by New Harbinger Publications.

To get you started using visualization to improve your memory, we will begin with a primer explaining some of the ways and reasons this technique is so effective for memory. Like elaboration, visualization is another means by which you can enhance the neural networks that store memories. In fact, you will find that visualization and elaboration are techniques that flow into one another quite readily. The imagination is an incredibly powerful tool, and the mind has an amazing ability to recreate images to a degree that can seem almost real.

When you visualize something, you not only place a picture of the thing into your mind's eye, you also add pseudosensory components to the information at hand. You are "seeing," "feeling," "smelling," and "touching" the thing you want to remember.

These visualized actions generate entire neural networks that would not have existed without the visualization process.

It is likely that you already know how to visualize, but it may not be a skill that you've practiced. For example, anytime you imagine the face of your child and you feel that you can actually "see" that face, you are visualizing. It is a fairly natural process.

However, to move this practice up to another level, there are some useful techniques you can employ. First, you will want to take a few minutes to sit still with your eyes closed and consciously try to visualize what you want to accomplish. This means you must reduce the distractions and take a time-out to remember. Many people will read this and think, "But I don't have the time for that. There is just no way." We will give you two responses to that.

First, it doesn't take more than a couple of minutes, and if you're so busy that you can't sit quietly and think for *two minutes*, then you need to seriously consider reducing the number of things you do. Second, think about all of the time you are going to waste later trying to remember. Think about the missed appointments, the forgotten item at the grocery store that you have to drive back to get. Think about how much time you spend looking for your keys. In the long run, you will be saving yourself time.

So, find a comfortable chair and sit quietly. Close your eyes and do five abdominal breaths. (If you have forgotten how to do this, look at the "Abdominal Breathing" exercise in chapter 3.) Once you have relaxed a bit, bring the information that you want to remember to your mind's eye. If it is an object, imagine it as fully as you can. Try and see it. Imagine all of its details. Does it have a scent? How does it feel to touch it? What emotions does it bring up for you? Does it have a taste? Zoom in and look at parts of the object, then zoom out and see the whole thing. If it is more than one object, bring the whole collection to mind. Look at the surroundings. Let your mind wander around like a handheld camera, analyzing all of the surrounding details. Imagine yourself in the same space with the object.

Once you are satisfied that you have fully envisioned what it is you want to remember to the best of your ability, slowly bring yourself back to reality. Sit for another moment in your chair before getting up to return to your ordinary day. Later, when it is time to remember, the visualization will certainly help you.

RETRIEVAL

As we've said previously, retrieval is the part of the memory process where people actually see their problems. When we want to pull information out of our brain and it "isn't there," we get frustrated and feel scared, ashamed, or just plain dumb.

As much as we like comparing the human brain to a computer or a filing system, it is actually far more sophisticated and complex than either of these. It is unfortunate but true that memory is not just a simple matter of filing information in a place where you can easily go and retrieve it whenever you want it. The mind is many, many orders of magnitude more complex than this. However, if you are conscious about it, you can use some of the ways your mind files information to your advantage for retrieving it.

ASSOCIATIVE RECALL

As you have learned throughout this book, the mind files information in many different places by many different themes.

One useful way to recall information is to use this system to your advantage and go in through the back door in order to remember (Mason and Kohn 2001).

If you can't seem to find the information you are looking for, bring to mind some of the associated memories that might come up with it. For example, if you can't seem to remember your colleague's wife's name, bring your colleague and his name to mind instead. This may lead the way back to the memory you are actually trying to get at, and will save you the frustration and the wasted time of concentrating to the point of obsession on the information you are trying to retrieve.

This technique is particularly useful if you try to recall something associated with a piece of information already strongly encoded in your memory. In the example above, we suggested that you use your colleague's name to remember his wife's name. The rationale behind this is that your colleague's name already has a sufficiently strong neural pathway in your mind. By calling up that pathway, you can more easily find traces of the other memory.

In most cases, there are tons of associated information that you can contemplate to get at the memory you are trying to recall. Be creative and open-minded and this strategy should help out quite a bit.

CONTEXT AND STATE-DEPENDENT MEMORIES

Nearly everyone has had the experience of walking out of the living room and into the kitchen only to forget what they wanted there and why they even left the comfort of the couch in the first place (unless it was to restore some circulation to their legs). Then, when they return to the living room, the reason for going into the kitchen suddenly pops back into their mind. This is called a *state-dependent memory*.

States in which you formulate information to be remembered, however, can be more complex than simply returning to the place where the memory was created. For example, if you were happy while you were encoding the information, it is more likely that you will remember the information when you are in the "state" of happiness.

When you are having a difficult time trying to call a piece of information to mind, try remembering the emotional state you were in when you encoded the information. Think about the emotion you were having, the physical surroundings you were in, or your frame of mind at the time. Recreating the state in which you encoded the memory may lead you on the path back to the memory itself.

Also, remember that memories are created in larger contexts. Time, emotions, personal history, and social events all play a part in the creation of a memory. If you can't get back to a piece of information easily, try framing the information in the context in which it was remembered. For example, try thinking about the time of day, how you were feeling, or what happened to you that day to retrieve the memory you are trying to locate. Is there a story tied up in the memory? Did something important or funny or strange happen? Any of these contexts can lead you back to the information you're trying to remember.

> **TIP:** Remember to relax while encoding and retrieving information. If you haven't yet explored chapter 3, you may want to do so now. Use any of the relaxation strategies described there to help you relax while you encode and recall.

YOUR EXPERIENCE IS THE TEST

Although we have stated this quite a lot, we would like to say it again: None of these techniques will work unless you use them. Reading about techniques to enhance memory isn't going to get you anywhere. You need to take this information with you outside the pages of this book and make it work for you.

Your experience is the ultimate test. There are a number of suggested strategies to enhance your memory in this chapter (and there will be quite a few more as the book progresses). Use what works for you. Don't worry, you won't hurt our feelings if you don't use all of the techniques in this book. Take them with you, try them out, and use the ones that work for you. Forget about the others.

If there are techniques you don't like because you tried them out and they didn't work for you, you can tear out the pages they are written on if you wish. We will never know.

6

The Truth about Herbs, Supplements, and Alternative Treatments

One of the biggest misconceptions regarding the use of herbal products and supplements is that they are much safer than medications prescribed by a doctor. This widespread belief about the safety of these products is based on the fact that many people choose to take advice from their friends rather than make an appointment with a qualified doctor.

How many times have you found yourself at the supermarket, your kid's baseball game, or even at a family gathering trying

> **YOU MUST BE CAREFUL ABOUT WHERE YOU RECEIVE YOUR INFORMATION.**

to deal with your Cousin Joe's advice on the herbal product he thinks is best for your painful ingrown toenail? Of course, this is an exaggeration; however, we would bet that you can recall at least one instance in which you sought advice from an ill-equipped individual about an aspect of your health or well-being. This is not to say that there are no safe and effective herbal medications on the market for your health concerns. It is to say that you must be careful about where you receive your information.

In this chapter, you will learn about some of the herbal, supplemental, and alternative treatments that supposedly help to improve memory. You will also learn about some herbs you should avoid rather than incorporating them into your "memory regimen." However, before discussing any herbs or supplements, there are some things you should understand to get the full benefit of this chapter, and the following one on prescribed medications.

First, the material in both chapters 6 and 7 is based on clinical studies that were all conducted in the past few decades. Since all of the information we have regarding the efficacy and safety of herbal treatments and supplements is derived from clinical trials, let's be sure you understand exactly what clinical trials are.

Merriam-Webster's Collegiate Dictionary (11th edition) defines a clinical trial as "a scientifically controlled study of the safety and effectiveness of a therapeutic agent (as a drug or vaccine) using consenting human subjects." Clinical trials are the gold standard on which health professionals rely for evidence-based practices regarding the safety and efficacy of medications or products. However, because these studies are conducted in controlled settings, the "real-world" use of these products may vary between individual patients. That's why it is essential that you follow the instructions of your doctor, pharmacist, or the package label when taking such products.

Another concern you should have when considering using herbal and nutritional supplements is that they are poorly monitored when compared to the meticulous regulatory process that prescribed medications must undergo. Although it is likely that stricter regulations on nonprescription products eventually will be put in place, you must understand that there is currently a vast difference between herbal and prescribed medications when it comes to the laws of our federal government.

Therefore, we are presented with a number of distinct problems when considering the quality of nonprescription products. First of all, the packaging on these products doesn't always reflect the entire set of ingredients that have been compounded in the product. Also, the manufacturers of these products are not required to provide evidence regarding the safety or efficacy of the product. For that reason, common drug interactions and side effects are seldom known, which can lead to a number of potential cascading events that might affect other aspects of your health. Furthermore, the manufacturing centers of these products are neither inspected nor monitored by the Food and Drug Administration (FDA).

Having said all that, we also want to say that there are many herbal products and supplements that have been independently studied and found to be efficacious for treating many types of conditions. Many vitamins, hormones, herbs, nutritional supplements, and alternative medications claim to improve your memory. We will now take an in-depth look at some of these products.

Hopefully, you will gain some clarity as to which products to consider as possible additions to your "memory regimen" and which products to consider as part of your "ancient memory."

GINKGO BILOBA

Ginkgo biloba, one of a class of nutritional supplements referred to as *phytomedicinal* (meaning medicines derived from plants), is one of the most widely sought supplements on the market today. The leaves and seeds of this tree provide the extract Egb, which has been shown to provide benefit to vital organs such as your heart, lungs, and brain. The concentration of this compound is at its highest in autumn when the ginkgo's leaves begin to change color. Note that formulations of ginkgo biloba contain only about 2 percent of the Egb extract in the final product.

In the last decade or so, there have been a number of studies about ginkgo's role in improving health. One research study conducted by the Bronfman Science Center in Massachusetts and published in the New England Journal of Medicine studied 98 men and 132 women, splitting them into two groups of 115 (Solomon et al. 2002). One group received 40 milligrams of ginkgo biloba three times a day for six weeks, while the other group received a placebo for the same time period. Two hundred and three of these subjects completed the six-week regimen. The results of the study indicated that ginkgo biloba did not enhance the "cognitive function of learning, memory, attention, and concentration or naming and verbal fluency in elderly adults without cognitive impairment" (Solomon et al. 2002, 835).

Another study, conducted by the New York University Medical Center and the Memory Centers of America, concluded that patients with very mild to moderate forms of dementia showed improvement with ginkgo, while severely demented patients demonstrated only a slowing down in the progression of their disease (Le Bars et al. 2002).

There have not been a clinically significant number of reported drug interactions for those using ginkgo; however, it should be used with caution due to its antiplatelet effects in patients who are taking anticoagulation medications. Although there are no requirements to report side effects for herbal medications, there have been some commonly reported adverse effects, including mild gastrointestinal upset, gas, nausea/vomiting, headaches, and diarrhea.

Bottom line: Ginkgo may slow down brain damage from progressive dementias. Research also shows that it may provide some mild improvements in cognitive functioning for those suffering from Alzheimer's disease and other progressive dementias. It may also help correct some lapses and changes in cognition caused by normal aging. Ginkgo will not boost memory or enhance cognitive functioning and it is certainly not a miracle IQ enhancer. It is a proven antioxidant that will help to prevent rather than cure memory impairment.

ESTROGEN

As if enduring monthly menstruation, pregnancy, childbirth, risk of breast cancer, and menopause wasn't enough, some research indicates that postmenopausal women have a greater risk of developing Alzheimer's disease than elderly men do. This has created an increasing controversy as to whether women are at a greater risk of developing dementia.

Doctor Gayatri Devi, from the New York Memory and Healthy Aging Services, has created a Web site on women and Alzheimer's disease. She finds that among estrogen's effects on women's mood, attention, and language skills are also effects on postmenopausal patients' memories. She says there are estrogen "docking sites" present throughout the brain and that when they are activated, they stimulate memory. Moreover, she says that estrogen increases the presence of some neurotransmitters in the brain, such as acetylcholine, which has been associated with stimulating memory and muscle functioning. Because of the decline in estrogen after women go through menopause, their chances of developing Alzheimer's disease do indeed increase (Devi 2004).

This leads us into the increasingly complex area of replacing the estrogen that is lost. You might think it would be a simple fix just to give estrogen tablets to postmenopausal women and thus prevent memory loss; however, it's not that easy. Several clinical trials conducted in recent years indicate estrogen replacement in postmenopausal patients is actually contraindicated. The Women's Health Initiative Memory Study (Espeland et al. 2004) found that women receiving conjugated equine estrogen demonstrated an increased risk for dementia. The study also showed that hormone replacement therapy was not only ineffective for dementia but that it actually caused detrimental effects to patients' health.

On the other hand, a study conducted at the University of Southern California (Brinton 2004) concluded that estrogen therapy enhances "neurological health" and prevents or alleviates Alzheimer's disease. So how are we supposed to know which study is accurate? Well, that's the same question the researchers at the University of Southern California asked themselves after seeing the results from the Women's Health Initiative Memory Study. They performed a follow-up study, which indicated that both of the studies were accurate. This time, the researchers at the University of Southern California said that if estrogen replacement therapy were begun in the early stages of postmenopause when the neurons are still healthy, it did indeed decrease the risk for developing Alzheimer's disease. Also, its efficacy depends on the type of progestin in the hormone replacement combination.

Bottom line: Estrogen is one of the most intensely studied hormones affecting memory impairment. Well-controlled studies have demonstrated mixed results. There seems to be some agreement that the earlier it is used the better. It has been shown to delay the onset of Alzheimer's disease, but not to improve memory. When combined with progesterone, side effects can be serious, including an increased risk for breast cancer.

VITAMIN E

Vitamin E is one of the fat-soluble vitamins essential for life. It can be found in some types of vegetables and in grains, fruits, meats, eggs, fish, and oils. This indispensable vitamin has demonstrated clinically significant antioxidant properties. Antioxidants have the ability to destroy neurotoxic free radicals created during normal metabolic processes. Free radicals are atoms or groups of atoms with an odd (unpaired) number of electrons and can be formed when oxygen interacts with certain molecules. Once formed these highly reactive radicals can start a chain reaction, like dominoes. The chief danger comes from the damage they can do when they react with important cellular components such as DNA, or the cell membrane. Cells may function poorly or die if this occurs. These free radicals have been widely studied in recent years and have been found to be an important cause of cognitive degeneration in Alzheimer's disease and even mild cognitive impairment (*Clinical Pharmacology* 2004).

This link between vitamin E and Alzheimer's disease has sparked numerous clinical trials to challenge this remarkable discovery. Unfortunately, most of the studies found that taking a vitamin E supplement may be beneficial only if consumption begins at the very early stages of dementia.

For example, in 2004, the School of Medicine at the University of Pennsylvania published the results of a double-blind study that supported their hypothesis that antioxidant therapy, given to older mice, did not show a clinically significant difference when compared to the placebo given (Sung et al. 2004). Also, the School of Medicine at Duke University has published an article stating there is no evidence that vitamin E can serve as preventative therapy in patients who are not yet experiencing Alzheimer's disease (Burke and Morgenlander 1999).

Before these studies, it was thought that a maximum dose of 2000 IU (international units) taken throughout the day would provide beneficial effects to memory. However, this high a dose could create a bleeding problem in patients who suffer from a vitamin K deficiency. Also, it could have negative effects on the thyroid, adrenal hormones, immune responses, and sexual performance. Note that there have been similar findings with vitamins C and B as well.

Bottom line: Vitamin E has been shown to be one of the most effective and efficient antioxidants on the market. It has been shown to act against toxic byproducts (free radicals) deposited in the brain. Vitamin E assists with the destruction of neurotoxic free radicals created by oxidative metabolism. Originally, the recommended dose to address memory problems was as high as 2000 IU. It is now thought that much lower doses will have the same effect with significantly decreased side effects. Although many well-controlled studies have reported conflicting results, vitamin E is still one of the best choices of natural supplements for addressing good memory maintenance.

B VITAMINS

Vitamins B_1 (thiamine), B_6 (pyridoxine), B_9 (folic acid), and B_{12} (cyanocobalamin) have all been suggested, in one way or another, to play a role in memory function. B_1 is a water-soluble vitamin found in yeast, cereal grains, legumes, peas, pork, and beef. It has been studied in children by Columbia University in New York and found to increase reaction time and stimulate memory. There is no credible evidence yet to suggest that adults should use thiamine for the improvement of memory or to prevent memory loss. B_6 is also a water-soluble vitamin found in cereal grains, legumes, liver, meat, eggs, and vegetables. It mainly is associated with mood control. There have been some anecdotal accounts as to its effect on memory, but only subjective correlations between the two. B_6 is found in yeast, liver, kidneys, and green leafy vegetables. B_{12} is found in meat and certain types of fish. When a declining memory is present, the possibility of decreased B_6 and B_{12} levels is among the first clinical considerations. This is the groundwork for many ongoing studies.

Bottom line: The B vitamins can prove dangerous if levels become too high. Consult your physician or pharmacist before beginning to take these as supplements to your normal nutrition.

GARLIC

Garlic is among the most studied herbal supplements available on the market today. Its medically active constituent, allicin, is derived from the bulb of *Allium sativum,* which has been used since the early Egyptian and Chinese dynasties. More than a thousand articles written over the past twenty years have been published about its potential effectiveness against infections, high blood glucose and cholesterol, neurotoxic free radicals, and clot formation. However, throughout many years of study, a strong correlation between the consumption of garlic and improved memory performance has not been established.

Bottom line: Garlic does contain some components that may assist memory functioning. Although there has not been a proven direct correlation between garlic and memory enhancement, it is worth trying. It may help and it will do no harm.

CHOLINE AND LECITHIN

There has been some speculation that patients suffering from dementia do not have the ability to convert choline to acetylcholine in the brain. As mentioned earlier, in the section dealing with estrogen, acetylcholine is an important neurotransmitter in muscle and memory functioning. Choline is just one component of a substance known as lecithin. As with the other products discussed in this chapter, there have been numerous clinical trials to determine if lecithin or choline would retard the progression of the different stages of dementia.

One study conducted by researchers at Duke University Medical Center found that using a high dose (20–35 grams per day) of lecithin did not slow the early onset of Alzheimer's disease (Heyman et al. 1987). The study had a total of thirty-seven qualified subjects. Lecithin was administered to sixteen of the subjects and a placebo was given to the remaining twenty-one people. The study's findings suggest that no differences were observed between the patients receiving lecithin and those given the placebo. In addition, the high doses that some believed might have improved or alleviated dementia could have caused side effects such as anorexia, excessive sweating and salivation, and gastrointestinal distress.

Bottom line: Acetylcholine has been identified as one of the primary neurotransmitters involved in cognitive functioning. Much of our current approach to treating memory impairment is to increase the level of acetylcholine available in the brain. Choline is one of the primary building blocks of acetylcholine and should therefore enhance the production of acetylcholine in the brain. This is the primary mechanism of action in most of the memory medications on the market that fall into the category of cholinesterase inhibitors (see chapter 7 for more details). The major problem with taking raw choline is that it has considerable difficulty crossing the blood-brain barrier and making its way into the brain.

CURCUMIN

Curcumin is an Indian spice found in the tropical plant turmeric. This spice gives American-style mustard and Indian curry their yellow color. Turmeric is thought to have significant effects as an anti-inflammatory, cancer-prevention agent, and memory stimulant. In 2001, the University of California at Los Angeles Department of Medicine and Neurology studied the effects of this spice (Frautschy et al. 2001). The study concluded that curcumin did suppress oxidative damage in rats. Studies are currently being conducted to determine how effective this spice is for humans.

Bottom line: Studies of this spice have revealed properties that seem to prevent structural correlations related to memory loss. The use of curcumin is primarily supported by the study done at the University of California at Los Angeles. The study suggested that curcumin reduces brain changes related to memory loss. The results also suggest that curcumin assists in removing *amyloid* (a starchlike protein complex associated with a variety of chronic diseases) from the brain. Curcumin has limited side effects, so its combined antioxidant and anti-inflammatory properties should prove helpful.

COENZYME Q_{10}

Coenzyme Q_{10}, discovered in 1957 at the University of Wisconsin, comes from beef heart and seafood. It is thought to be involved in supplying the neurons in the body with energy. It has been suggested that this fat-soluble antioxidant may protect the brain from the natural aging processes. However, its main claim to fame is its beneficial effects on the heart.

Bottom line: Coenzyme Q_{10} is an essential part of our diet that is now used medicinally to treat a long list of conditions where lack of energy and poor nutrition are implicated. Its mechanism of action strongly suggests that, potentially, it could play an important role in preventing neurological decline; however, further studies are needed to prove or disprove this speculation.

OTHER HERBAL AND NUTRITIONAL SUPPLEMENTS

There are other herbal and nutritional supplements worthy of note. Huperzine, an extract from Chinese club moss, has been shown to provide benefits to patients with a progressed stage of memory loss. It provides little to no benefit to patients with mild-to-moderate cases of memory loss. Selenium is a trace element that has been shown to have beneficial effects on brain function. It is found in garlic and is credited for garlic's effects on memory. (See the section on garlic above for more information.)

ALTERNATIVE TREATMENTS

In addition to the herbal and nutritional supplements that we have covered thus far, there are other treatments available that may help to improve your memory. These range from high blood pressure and cholesterol medications to vaccines and antibiotics. For the remainder of this chapter you will learn why, and why not, vaccines and antibiotics may potentially protect your memory. In chapter 7, which discusses prescription medications, you will learn more about the high blood pressure and cholesterol medications that may have beneficial effects on memory.

VACCINES

Certain types of memory disorders are associated with the progressive accumulation of proteins (A beta) in the brain that can lead to immune responses, which trigger a cascade of harmful events. These are the grounds for investigating the use of vaccines to prevent memory deterioration. According to *Merriam-Webster's Collegiate Dictionary* (11th edition), vaccines are "a preparation of killed microorganisms, living attenuated organisms, or fully virulent organisms that is administered to produce or artificially increase immunity to a particular disease." Some researchers believe that if it was possible to induce the immune reaction caused by the accumulation of proteins in the brain, that would be a very important step in the direction of preventing memory impairment.

Vaccines are used to create the undesired immune response before it occurs naturally in order to prevent future memory impairments. This is like being injected with the flu vaccine to prevent you from catching the flu. This is a relatively new concept; numerous studies are in the works but are still to come. There was one clinical study in which patients received the Abeta vaccination; however, some patients suffered from severe inflammation of the brain, causing the suspension of the trial (Broytman and Malter 2004). The study was by no means a waste of time, but merely the spirited beginning for future studies and formulations on the Abeta vaccination.

Bottom line: Vaccines are an exciting and very promising development that, in the future, potentially may be the key that opens the lock for memory loss.

SHOULD YOU TRY AN HERBAL MEDICATION OR NUTRITIONAL SUPPLEMENT?

It's important for you to weigh the benefits versus the risks when considering the use of herbal products and supplements. The claim that because they can be purchased without a doctor's prescription means they are safe enough to use unsupervised has plagued many professional health-care providers for decades. The truth of the matter is that these products are not regulated by the FDA and potentially could be harmful to your health if taken inappropriately.

There are many herbal products, supplements, and alternative treatments available to you for the treatment and prevention of memory loss, including ginkgo biloba, estrogen, vitamins,

> WEIGH THE BENEFITS VERSUS THE RISKS WHEN CONSIDERING THE USE OF HERBAL PRODUCTS AND SUPPLEMENTS.

garlic, lecithin, curcumin, and perhaps the use of vaccines. As you've read, many clinical studies have been conducted to determine the effectiveness of these products for improving memory. On the whole, most of the available studies do not support using herbal products and supplements as a reliable means to bring about a "miracle memory." However, if taken appropriately, several of these products can provide beneficial effects for other aspects of your health.

7

Prescription Medications That Affect Your Memory

Now, let's imagine a perfect world for a moment. Suppose you've started to notice that your memory is not as keen as it used to be and you visit your doctor for a consultation about it. Instead of the usual time-consuming neurological tests and the painful needle pricks to determine the precise treatment or exercises for your condition, the doctor prescribes a new state-of-the-art medication for you. For our purposes, let's call this medication "Instamem." The doctor tells you, "Just take one tablet of Instamem every morning before breakfast, and you should soon start seeing improvements in your memory."

Let's suppose that you've followed your doctor's instructions and a week later you start remembering things you haven't remembered for decades. At your follow-up appointment, you tell your doctor that you can now remember the name of your first girlfriend or boyfriend, your home phone number as a child, or even your third-grade teacher's name, the one who always scolded you for not sitting still in your seat during the math lesson.

Okay, let's return to reality now. The development of a medication that would stimulate childhood memories, like Instamem, is a big stretch. It's still beyond all our technological skills, at least for now. There are, however, new medications becoming available that have halted or slowed the progression of memory loss.

The purpose of this chapter is to give you a basic understanding of the medications currently available to you that can have either positive or negative effects on your memory. In this chapter, we will also take a look at some medications, such as cholesterol and blood pressure medications, that have been speculated about as having the ability to improve memory. Although most of the research on these medications is performed with the more severe and chronic forms of memory impairment (e.g., Alzheimer's disease), many parallels in how the mechanism of action might improve less severe memory challenges can still be drawn. The treatment of memory loss, no matter how mild it is, offers an exciting prospect for the future.

> NEW MEDICATIONS ARE BECOMING
> AVAILABLE THAT HAVE HALTED
> OR SLOWED THE PROGRESSION
> OF MEMORY LOSS.

Before we go any further into this chapter, there are a few things that must be addressed for you to benefit from the information presented here. As with chapter 6 on herbal and nutritional supplements, this chapter is based primarily on many clinical trials that were conducted in recent years.

Medication management is a principal component of your medical care. It is vitally important to select one physician as your primary care doctor who will coordinate your care and understand all aspects of your health condition. Also, don't be afraid to visit your local drugstore pharmacist with any concerns you may have regarding the use of your medications. Whomever you rely on to help you with managing your medication, that person must be aware of the names and dosages of all the medications and supplements you are currently taking.

Also, it might be helpful to prepare in advance a list of your medications and any questions you might have for your doctor before your next scheduled visit. Many of us suffer from what can be called the "white coat syndrome." In this syndrome, people frequently become very anxious and nervous when interviewed by a doctor wearing a white lab coat. Such nervousness sometimes causes us to forget to ask important questions that we would have otherwise asked.

SIDE EFFECTS ASSOCIATED WITH MEDICATIONS

Every drug on the market carries the potential for causing side effects as well as whatever benefit it confers. For this reason, when a doctor must select a patient-specific medication for any memory condition, potential side effects must also be considered. If the risks of developing serious side effects, or adverse reactions, from the medication outweigh the benefits, then it is unlikely that medication is the best choice for that patient.

Possible side effects of each medication covered in this chapter are listed. However, it is important to understand that not all side effects are listed here and even if a side effect is mentioned here, that doesn't mean you will develop it. In contrast to the herbal and nutritional products discussed in chapter 6, prescription medications are both regulated and regularly monitored by the FDA. Therefore, drug interactions and side effects are required by law to be reported to the FDA.

MEMORY-ENHANCING MEDICATIONS

Research is continuing on medications to improve memory and cognitive functioning. Overall, the reality today is that although the available medications may help to improve memory or to slow the progress of cognitive decline, these medications cannot reverse existing deficits. Generally, when we think of memory-enhancing medications, our thoughts go to the medications developed for Alzheimer's disease. Although most of the studies on memory have been conducted on people with diseases such as Alzheimer's, some of these medications are often prescribed for other forms of mild cognitive impairment.

Memory-enhancing medications fall into several classes of drugs. These are cholinesterase inhibitors, NMDA receptor antagonists, and ergot alkaloids, to mention but three. First we will discuss the class of cholinesterase inhibitors, which were the pioneers of these memory medications.

CHOLINESTERASE INHIBITORS

Most of the memory medications currently accepted by medical practitioners are cholinesterase inhibitors. These have been shown to slow down the progression of memory deterioration and to restore the ability to handle the cognitive aspects of daily activities.

As stated above, these medications will not stop or cure progressive memory problems, but they have demonstrated the ability to alleviate some problems with memory. Cholinesterase inhibitors act by increasing the amount of acetylcholine in the brain. Acetylcholine is believed to be important for memory and learning capabilities. Now we will take an in-depth look at some of the medications that belong to this class of drugs.

TACRINE

In 1993, tacrine, also known as Cognex, was the first drug approved for the treatment of symptoms associated with dementia, including impaired abilities in language use, reasoning, memory, and focused attention. Tacrine inhibits acetylcholinesterase, the enzyme that breaks down acetylcholine, and, as stated above, acetylcholine is believed to be essential for cognitive functions. Unfortunately, tacrine therapy has also been associated with liver dysfunction. Furthermore, the medication must be taken four times a day, which is another reason that patients have difficulty staying with a tacrine regimen.

Also, according to Maltby and colleagues (1994), a double-blind clinical trial in which tacrine was given to patients with mild-to-moderate symptoms of Alzheimer's disease found that tacrine provided no benefit to these patients. However, five years after that study, Mayeux and Sano (1999) found an average of 4.5 percent improvement in cognitive functioning following treatment with tacrine.

Side effects: The most commonly reported side effects include liver dysfunction, nausea/vomiting, diarrhea, myalgia, and ataxia. Less common side effects include anorexia, constipation, gas, dry mouth, indigestion, anxiety, hallucinations, and agitation. Cardiovascular side effects are uncommon.

Bottom line: Tacrine is ineffective for curing or stopping the progression of memory loss. However, it has been proven to slow down the progression of memory loss. At present, this is not a bad option, considering that it does provide some limited clinical benefit.

DONEPEZIL

Donepezil, also known as Aricept, was the second cholinesterase inhibitor approved by the FDA for the treatment of dementia. It has been used for patients with mild-to-moderate dementia conditions to decrease the associated symptoms. Donepezil is the most widely prescribed medication of its kind because it has not been associated with liver dysfunction and has to be administered only once a day.

The Medical Center at Duke University has made donepezil the focal point for one of its many studies (Krishnan et al. 2003). This double-blind study administered either donepezil or a placebo for twenty-four weeks to sixty-seven patients with mild-to-moderate Alzheimer's disease. For the first twenty-eight days, 5 milligrams of donepezil was administered daily, then 10 milligrams a day after that. The results clearly showed that the patients who received donepezil drug therapy had clinically significant improvement in their cognitive scores when compared to the patients who received the placebo.

Side effects: At 5 milligrams per day, donepezil is relatively well tolerated. The majority of side effects are seen at the initiation of drug therapy and at higher doses. The most commonly seen side effects include fatigue, nausea/vomiting, diarrhea, anorexia, and muscle cramping. Nausea/vomiting and diarrhea are frequently reported when patients stop taking the medication. Less common side effects include a decline in understanding language, bloating, chest pain, aggression, dizziness, and urinary incontinence.

Bottom line: Donepezil definitely provides beneficial effects for decreasing the symptoms associated with mild-to-moderate conditions of dementia. It is considered superior to tacrine because it has fewer side effects and more convenient dosing intervals. It is being used to treat milder forms of memory loss.

RIVASTIGMINE

Rivastigmine, also known as Exelon, is one of the newest cholinesterase inhibitors. It was introduced in 2000. To receive therapeutic benefit, a twice-daily dose is required. It has been administered to and studied in more five thousand patients from many different countries. The School of Medicine at Indiana University conducted a study to determine whether the response to rivastigmine is related to the severity of cognitive impairment

(Farlow et al. 2001). This was a nationwide study that concluded there is indeed a correlation between the two. Patients suffering from a more rapidly progressing disease state responded better to treatment with rivastigmine than did patients who were experiencing a slower progression of cognitive impairment.

Side effects: Unfortunately, the dose at which clinical benefit is seen (greater than or equal to 6 milligrams per day) is also the dosage at which side effects begin to appear. The more commonly seen side effects include nausea/vomiting, anorexia, diarrhea, abdominal pain, constipation, dyspepsia, gas, and belching. Some of these side effects can be decreased if rivastigmine is taken with food. To date, no liver dysfunction has been reported.

Bottom line: Rivastigmine has been proven to provide clinical benefit for up to two years in patients who suffer from a more rapidly progressing form of dementia. Unfortunately, this drug is an unlikely option for treating milder forms of forgetfulness.

GALANTAMINE

Galantamine, also known as Reminyl, is derived from the plant *Galanthus nivalis*. A six-month study at the University of Washington concluded that galantamine at 24 milligrams per day significantly improved overall brain functioning and cognition among Alzheimer's patients (Raskind et al. 2000).

Side effects: Galantamine should be administered with plenty of water and food to decrease side effects. The most common side effects include nausea/vomiting, diarrhea, abdominal pain, dyspepsia, dizziness, headache, decreased heart rate, and tremors.

Bottom line: Galantamine is similar to rivastigmine in that it acts as a cholinesterase inhibitor. It also requires a twice-daily administration and shows no harmful effects on the liver if taken at appropriate dosages.

NMDA Receptor Antagonists

The brain's N-methyl-D-aspartate (NMDA) receptors are important for memory and learning abilities. Overstimulation of NMDA receptors is thought to be one of the causes of Alzheimer's disease. When NMDA receptors are overstimulated by glutamate, the most profound excitatory neurotransmitter in the brain, it leads to neurological damage due to increased calcium concentrations in the brain's neurons. NMDA receptor antagonists are among the newer classes of medications to treat memory impairment.

Memantine

Memantine, also known as Namenda, is the first drug of its kind approved for the treatment of moderate-to-severe Alzheimer's disease. It is believed that memantine blocks the stimulating effects of glutamate. Like the cholinesterase inhibitors, memantine is not a cure for memory impairment or progressive dementias, but it can slow the progression of symptoms and help to improve memory functioning. The usual dosage is 10 milligrams twice daily. The School of Medicine at New York University conducted a twenty-eight-week study on memantine for the treatment of mild-to-severe forms of dementia (Reisberg et al. 2003). The study concluded that memantine exhibits few adverse effects and actually reduces clinical deterioration in patients.

Side effects: As the study indicated, memantine appears to be relatively well tolerated. The most common side effects include insomnia, agitation, headache, fatigue, pain, confusion, drowsiness, and hallucinations. Minimal cardiovascular events have been reported with the use of memantine.

Bottom line: NMDA receptor antagonists are new and promising agents in the treatment of memory disorders. Today, memantine is the only NMDA receptor antagonist approved by the FDA for use with Alzheimer's disease patients. It has relatively few side effects and is an exciting new development for this class of medications. It also has relatively few drug interactions and can be combined with cholinesterase inhibitors for synergistic effects.

ERGOT ALKALOIDS

Ergot alkaloids have an entirely different type of mechanism than cholinesterase inhibitors and NMDA receptor antagonists. For this class of drugs, the information about how they work is largely based on animal studies. It is thought that ergot alkaloids work by means of increasing the uptake of oxygen and improving neuronal cell metabolism while correcting low levels of specific neurotransmitters in the brain. Future directions for this class of medications indicate promising results for the treatment of memory loss.

ERGOLOID MESYLATES

Ergoloid mesylates, also known as Hydergine, are used in combination with other medications for the treatment of cognitive impairment in older individuals. They have been around since the early 1950s. The studies conducted on ergoloid mesylates have had conflicting results. Thompson and colleagues, in an article published in the *New England Journal of Medicine* (1990), demonstrated that no differences were seen in patients taking ergoloid mesylates compared to patients taking a placebo. On the other hand, a study in 1994 by Schneider and Olin found some improvements in the associated symptoms of dementia.

Side effects: Ergoloid mesylates have been associated with cardiovascular effects, including decreased heart rate and blood pressure. Other commonly reported side effects are headache, dizziness, fainting, and gastrointestinal symptoms (nausea/vomiting, anorexia, dyspepsia, and stomach cramping).

Bottom line: Ergot alkaloids warrant further investigative trials to determine their effectiveness for treating memory loss. Because of their large number of side effects and their lack of efficacy, ergoloid mesylates are not considered first-line agents for the enhancement or improvement of memory functioning.

OFF-LABEL MEDICATIONS

Off-label medications are medications prescribed by physicians to treat disease states other than those for which the medication received FDA approval. Several classes of medications have been suggested for off-label use because of their beneficial effects on cognitive impairment. We will take a brief look at statins, calcium channel blockers, NSAIDs (nonsteroidal anti-inflammatory agents), and antibiotics in the next section.

STATINS

Statins are medications used to lower cholesterol. Some examples of medications in this class include Lipitor (atorvastatin), Zocor (simvastatin), and Mevacor (lovastatin). High cholesterol has been found to have a significant correlation with the many causes of progressive dementia. The School of Medicine at Brown University (Scott and Laake 2001) conducted a study on statins to determine whether they reduce the risk of developing neuronal plaques (this "hardening" of the brain's neurons is one of the factors thought to contribute to memory loss as we age, and to more severe forms of memory loss, such as Alzheimer's disease, as well).

The researchers concluded that there is not enough evidence to recommend using statins to reduce the risk of Alzheimer's disease, but that there is evidence that statins do play a role in slowing the progression of the disease (Scott and Laake 2001). Further research is needed on the use of statins for this condition.

CALCIUM CHANNEL BLOCKERS

Calcium channel blockers (CCBs), for example, verapamil, are used for a variety of cardiovascular conditions, including high blood pressure and chest pain. As mentioned earlier in this chapter in regard to the NMDA receptor antagonists, increased calcium levels in the brain coincide with cognitive decline. One would think that if the inward flow of calcium was blocked, that there would be a beneficial effect on neurological decline; however, many studies have found the opposite effect to occur.

A study performed at the University of Calgary suggests that people taking long-term doses of calcium channel blockers are at much greater risk for experiencing cognitive decline than those using other agents for cardiovascular health (Maxwell et al. 1999).

NSAIDs (Nonsteroidal Anti-Inflammatory Drugs)

Inflammation within the brain has also been implicated as one of the causes of memory loss and even of Alzheimer's disease. Certain neurons that process acetylcholine are particularly vulnerable to inflammation. Thus, nonsteroidal anti-inflammatory drugs, such as indomethacin and ibuprofen, have been used to treat such conditions. It is also believed that patients with chronic conditions due to inflammation, such as arthritis, have a lower risk of developing long-term memory impairment because of their long-term use of NSAIDs. As with other medications discussed in this chapter, we now turn to clinical trials to determine the reality about the results of using NSAIDs to cope with memory loss.

Researchers at the School of Medicine at the University of Brighton conducted a study of ibuprofen on this matter and concluded there is not enough evidence to recommend the use ibuprofen for the treatment of progressive memory decline. They even went so far as to state that the risks of side effects, such as bleeding, outweigh any benefit that NSAIDS could offer to patients suffering loss of memory (Tabet and Feldmand 2003).

ANTIBIOTICS

The last off-label medications to discuss are antibiotics. The term "antibiotics" is a very broad umbrella under which many different classes of drugs used for treating many types of infections are grouped. The class of antibiotics that is of interest to us is called "chelators." Clioquinol is an example of a chelating antibiotic, one that crosses the blood-brain barrier and has a relatively high affinity for zinc and copper ions in the brain. A study done at Duke University Medical Center found some association between zinc and copper levels and progressive memory decline such as Alzheimer's disease. Currently, a double-blind clinical trial is being conducted to study the use of clioquinol in combination with vitamin B_{12}. This study may provide us with new information that may lead to new treatments for memory loss (Finefrock et al. 2003).

MEDICATIONS WITH A NEGATIVE EFFECT ON MEMORY

The final part of this chapter lists medications that potentially could affect your memory in a negative way (*Physician's Desk Reference* 2001; Sabiston 1997; Preston, O'Neil, and Talaga 1999). This list was also published in an earlier book by one of our authors called *The Memory Workbook* (Mason and Kohn 2001). Keep in mind that these medications can have negative effects either directly or indirectly. They are listed in alphabetic order and their generic names can be found within the parentheses. This list will help you check out your own medications to see whether they might be implicated in your memory loss. It is also very important to bear in mind this fact: Every patient is affected differently by medication.

MEDICATIONS THAT MAY LEAD TO MEMORY IMPAIRMENT

There are medications on the market to treat specific medical conditions that have a detrimental effect on your memory. If you believe a medication that has been prescribed to you is impairing your memory, discuss this medication with your doctor. It is possible that the medication or dosage can be altered. Below is a sample of medications that may be negatively impacting your memory.

EVERY PATIENT IS AFFECTED
DIFFERENTLY BY MEDICATION.

BLOOD PRESSURE MEDICATIONS

- Aldactazide (spironolactone)
- Aldomet (methyldopa)
- Aldoril (methyldopa)
- Apresazide (hydralazine/HCTZ)
- Apresoline (hydralazine HCl)
- Atropine
- Blocadren (timolol)
- Bumex (bumetanide)
- Cartrol (carteolol)
- Combipres (clonidine)
- Coreg (carvedilol)
- Corgard (nadolol)
- Corzide (bendroflumethiazide)
- Demadex (torsemide)
- Diupres (reserpine)
- Diuril (chlorothiazide)
- Dyazide (triamterene)
- Enduron (methyclothiazide)
- Enduronyl (deserpidine)
- Esidrix (hydrochlorothiazide)
- Hydropres (reserpine)

- Hygroton (chlorthalidone)
- Inderal (propranolol)
- Inderide LA (propranolol)
- Kerlone (betaxolol)
- Levatol (penbutolol)
- Lopressor (metoprolol)
- Lozol (indapamide)
- Metahydrin (trichlormethiazide)
- Moduretic (amiloride)
- Normodyne (labetalol)
- Regroton (reserpine)
- Salutensin (reserpine)
- Sectral (acebutolol)
- Ser-Ap-Es (reserpine)
- Tenoretic (atenolol)
- Tenormin (atenolol)
- Visken (pindolol)
- Zaroxolyn (metolazone)
- Zebeta (bisoprolol)
- Ziac (bisoprolol)

PSYCHIATRIC AND NEUROLOGICAL MEDICATIONS

- Atarax/Vistaril (hydroxyzine)
- Ativan (lorazepam)
- BuSpar (buspirone)
- Butisol Sodium (butabarbital)
- Centrax (prazepam)
- Compazine (prochlorperazine)
- Dalmane (flurazepam)
- Doriden (glutethimide)
- Elavil (amitriptyline)
- Equanil (meprobamate)
- Halcion (triazolam)
- Haldol (haloperidol)
- Klonopin (clonazepam)
- Librium (chlordiazepoxide)
- Luminal Sodium (phenobarbital)

- Mellaril (thioridazine)
- Miltown (meprobamate)
- Navane (thiothixene)
- Nembutal (pentobarbital)
- Noctec (chloral hydrate)
- Noludar (methyprylon)
- Prolixin (fluphenazine)
- Restoril (temazepam)
- Serax (oxazepam)
- Stelazine (trifluoperazine)
- Thorazine (chlorpromazine)
- Tranxene (clorazepate)
- Valium (diazepam)
- Xanax (alprazolam)

STOMACH MEDICATIONS

- Axid (nizatidine)
- Pepcid (famotidine)

- Tagamet (cimetidine)
- Zantac (ranitidine)

MEDICATIONS THAT MAY LEAD TO CONFUSION

Medications listed below may cause mental confusion. As with any medication, it is important to discuss possible side effects with your physician.

CARDIAC MEDICATIONS

- Catapres (clonidine HCl)
- digitalis diuretics
- Duraquin (quinidine)
- Dura-Tabs (quinidine)
- Lanoxicap (digoxin)
- Lanoxin (digoxin)

- Lidocaine
- Norpace (disopyramide phosphate)
- Reserpine
- Tenex (guanfacine HCl)

ANTIBIOTICS

- Chibroxin (norfloxacin)
- Ciloxan/Cipro (ciprofloxacin)
- Cytovene (ganciclovir)
- Levaquin (levofloxacin)
- Maxaquin (lomefloxacin)
- Ocuflox/Floxin (ofloxacin)
- Penetrex (enoxacin)

- Raxar (grepafloxacin)
- Symmetrel (amantadine HCl)
- Urised (methenamine/ methylene blue/salol)
- Zagam (sparfloxacin)
- Zovirax (acyclovir)

DIABETES DRUGS

- Amaryl (glimepiride)
- DiaBeta/Micronase (glyburide)
- Diabinese (chlorpropamide)
- Dymelor (acetohexamide)
- Glucotrol (glipizide)

- Humalog (insulin lispro)
- insulin
- Orinase (tolbutamide)
- Tolinase (tolazamide)

SYSTEMIC MEDICATIONS

- Acthar (corticotropin)
- Azmacort (triamcinolone)
- Cortef (hydrocortisone)
- Cortone Acetate (cortisone)
- Decadron/Hexadrol (dexamethasone)

- Deltasone/Meticorten (prednisone)
- Diprolene/Valisone (betamethasone)
- Medrol (methylprednisolone)
- Metreton/Pred Forte (prednisolone acetate)

COLD AND ALLERGY MEDICATIONS

- Atarax/Vistaril (hydroxyzine HCl/pamoate)
- Benadryl (diphenhydramine)
- Chlor-Trimeton (chlorpheniramine maleate)
- Dimetane (brompheniramine maleate)
- Hismanal (astemizole)

- Myidil (triprolidine)
- Optimine (azatadine maleate)
- Periactin (cyproheptadine HCl)
- Seldane (terfenadine)
- Tavist-D (clemastine fumarate)
- Vistaril (hydroxyzine pamoate)

PAIN MEDICATIONS

- Advil/Motrin (ibuprofen)
- Aleve/Naprosyn (naproxen)
- Ansaid/Ocufen (flurbiprofen)
- Arthropan (choline salicylate)
- Ascriptin/Bufferin (aspirin)
- Bayer/Ecotrin (aspirin)
- Butazolidin (phenylbutazone)
- Clinoril (sulindac)
- Daypro (oxaprozin)
- Disalcid (salsalate)
- Doan's Pills (magnesium salicylate)
- Dolobid (diflunisal)
- Duract (bromfenac sodium)
- Feldene (piroxicam)

- general anesthesia
- Indocin (indomethacin)
- Lodine (etodolac)
- Meclomen (meclofenamate sodium)
- Nalfon (fenoprofen calcium)
- Orudis (ketoprofen)
- Relafen (nabumetone)
- Talwin (pentazocine/aspirin)
- Tolectin (tolmetin sodium)
- Toradol (ketorolac tromethamine)
- Trilisate (choline or magnesium salicylate)
- Voltaren (diclofenac sodium)

STOMACH MEDICATIONS

- Antivert (meclizine HCl)
- Atropine (atropine sulfate)
- Axid (nizatidine)
- Bentyl (dicyclomine HCl)
- Compazine (prochlorperazine)
- Donnatal (belladonna alkaloids/phenobarbital)
- Librax (clidinium/ chlordiazepoxide)

- Lomotil (diphenoxylate HCl/ atropine sulfate)
- Pepcid (famotidine)
- Phenergan (promethazine HCl)
- Tagamet (cimetidine)
- Tigan (trimethobenzamide HCl)
- Zantac (ranitidine)

ANTIDEPRESSANTS

- Asendin (amoxapine)
- Aventyl/Pamelor (nortriptyline)
- Desyrel (trazodone)
- Elavil (amitriptyline)
- Lithobid/Lithonate (lithium carbonate)
- Limbitrol (amitriptyline/ chlordiazepoxide)
- Ludiomil (maprotiline)

- Norpramin (desipramine)
- Prozac (fluoxetine)
- Sinequan (doxepin HCl)
- Surmontil (trimipramine)
- Tofranil (imipramine)
- Triavil (amitriptyline/ perphenazine)
- Wellbutrin (bupropion HCl)

SLEEPING PILLS, TRANQUILIZERS, AND HYPNOTICS

- Ativan (lorazepam)
- barbiturates
- BuSpar (buspirone HCl)
- Centrax (prazepam)
- Dalmane (flurazepam)
- Doriden (glutethimide)
- Halcion (triazolam)
- Librium (chlordiazepoxide)
- Miltown/Equanil (meprobamate)

- Noctec (chloral hydrate)
- Noludar (methyprylon)
- Restoril (temazepam)
- Serax (oxazepam)
- Tranxene (clorazepate)
- Valium (diazepam)
- Vistaril/Atarax (hydroxyzine pamoate)
- Xanax (alprazolam)

BARBITURATES

- Butisol (butabarbital)
- Luminal/Solfoton (phenobarbital)

- Nembutal (pentobarbital)

ANTIPSYCHOTICS

- Clozaril (clozapine)
- Haldol (haloperidol)
- Mellaril (thioridazine)
- Navane (thiothixene)
- Prolixin (fluphenazine)

- Reglan (metoclopramide)
- Stelazine (trifluoperazine)
- Thorazine (chlorpromazine)
- Triavil (amitriptyline/perphenazine)

NEUROLOGICAL MEDICATIONS

- Artane (trihexyphenidyl)
- Cogentin (benztropine)
- Dilantin (phenytoin sodium)
- Ergoset (bromocriptine)
- Klonopin (clonazepam)
- Larodopa (levodopa)

- Parlodel (bromocriptine mesylate)
- Permax (pergolide mesylate)
- phenobarbital
- Primidone (primidone)
- Sinemet (carbidopa/levodopa)
- Symmetrel (amantadine HCl)

OTHER MEDICATIONS

- Amipaque (metrizamide)
- Akineton (biperden)
- Anafranil (clomipramine HCl)
- Artane (trihexyphenidyl HCl)
- Cytosar-U (cytarabine)

- Elspar (asparaginase)
- Lioresal (baclofen)
- Mesoridazine (serentil)
- Oxybutin (oxybutin chloride)
- steroids

CONCLUDING REMARKS

Although it is highly unlikely that a medication with the properties of "Instamem" will ever be marketed, there are promising new developments for treating memory-related disorders.

The leading class of medications is classified as cholinesterase inhibitors. They work by preserving the neurotransmitter acetylcholine, which is definitely important for your memory and learning abilities. Tacrine, donepezil, rivastigmine, and galantamine are all cholinesterase inhibitors. Tacrine has a limited use because of its adverse effects on the liver. Donepezil is the most widely used in this class because of its convenient once-a-day dosing and limited effects on the liver. Rivastigmine provides clinical benefit for up to two years, while galantamine was found to improve cognitive and overall brain functioning.

NMDA receptor antagonists, a newly approved class of medications, have relatively few side effects or adverse drug interactions. This is important because it means they can be combined with cholinesterase inhibitors to provide synergistic effects to patients. Ergot alkaloids are an older class of medications used for memory loss; however, they have been shown to have many side effects and little clinical benefit.

A fair number of off-label medications have been tried for the treatment of memory loss. They include statins, calcium channel blockers, NSAIDs, and antibiotics. These medications, however, have not had a sufficient number of research studies conducted to warrant their use for the treatment of memory loss.

While some medications may enhance your memory, there are many that can actually cause memory decline. We have listed the majority of the medications that can affect your memory

WHILE SOME MEDICATIONS MAY ENHANCE YOUR MEMORY, THERE ARE MANY THAT CAN ACTUALLY CAUSE MEMORY DECLINE.

adversely. It would be a wise step to take the time to compare the medications you take regularly with this list.

It is important for you to understand that many ongoing clinical trials are taking place today for many other medications to help improve memory. Most of the medications listed in this chapter have been tested on more severe forms of memory loss, but it will be up to your physician to address your changes in memory at this chemical level, and to decide whether you are a good candidate for a particular medication.

8

Memory Tips, Tricks, Tools, and Tactics

Memories are a cherished part of our lives, whether we're reminiscing about funny or important family events, historical occasions, or the mundane daily routine. We all feel a lack of control and a sense of loss when we can't remember what we've set our hearts and minds on recalling. To help "cure" this fault, we have some memory tips and tricks to offer you in this chapter and we will give you the opportunity to practice some of these skills. We've categorized these tips and tricks so you can focus on a category that will fit your personality and thought processes. Even better, we've also developed some practical tips to assist you in determining whether you are more inclined to an intellectual approach or more oriented to using your body. Regardless of your personality or learning style, we're sure you'll find some useful tips, tricks, tools, and tactics in this chapter.

PRACTICAL MEMORY TIPS FOR ENCODING

Memory consists of three main components: encoding, storage, and retrieval. Both components are required to generate a memory. When your focus is directed at the encoding process, retrieval will come naturally. Knowledge is power and practical use of your knowledge of how memory works will greatly enhance your memory, and life in general.

Limit distractions: When you limit distractions, it will assist in learning new material and in enhancing your recall. It is much easier to pay attention if you are in a quiet environment free from distraction. If your spouse, friend, boss, or significant other wants to tell you something, then turn off the TV, radio, or your internal thoughts and focus on what is said to you. (If you are trying to

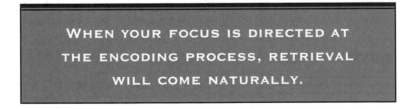

WHEN YOUR FOCUS IS DIRECTED AT THE ENCODING PROCESS, RETRIEVAL WILL COME NATURALLY.

watch a movie, then turn off your spouse, friend, boss, or significant other.) If you find you're having difficulty grasping what is being said, repeat the conversation back to the other person. If you are trying to recall something or maneuver your way somewhere, such as driving to a new or even familiar location, stop all conversation, especially phone conversation. Put your makeup or razor away and focus on where you are and where you're going.

Keep your windshield clean: It's difficult to see where you are going and to read street signs if your windows are dirty. Distractions as simple as hunger, tight apparel, or something in your eye are all disruptive and drain energy from focusing on the task at hand. Removing these types of distractions when you want to concentrate will lead to an improved memory.

Memory spot: Create a memory spot in your home or office. Find a container, such as a beautiful basket or a decorative crate, to stash all those important items you need before heading out of the door. These might include your calendar, directions, wallet or purse, glasses, keys, lists, and so on. Train yourself to check out your memory spot before you leave your house. Be consistent. It may take a while to train yourself to empty your pockets or purse and place the contents into your memory spot at the end of the day. But once you've established this as a new habit, it will be very helpful in your daily life. Also, you can create mobile memory spots. If you are a man, always put your keys in your right front pocket. If you are a woman, always carry your keys in your purse on the right side. If you always place important items on the same side, you will quickly develop the habit of looking on that side for important personal belongings.

Reminders for remembering: If you are in the middle of a task or out somewhere and you suddenly experience an "Oh, I need to . . ." moment, give yourself a reminder or a cue to remember this task. For example, switch the wrist you wear your watch on, or place a loose rubber band around your wrist, or turn a piece of jewelry in a different direction. Be sure to change the placement of something ordinary so it will stand out from your normal environment and thus serve as a useful reminder to remember to do the task you just remembered!

Verbalize: Give yourself spoken reminders to do a task. For instance, if you need to remember to care for your pets, say aloud, "Feed the cats. Meow meow meow." You will reinforce the encoding of this memory with verbal reinforcement as well as with a touch of humor. You will also increase the likelihood of completing this task, and your pet will be grateful. This trick also works for reminders like "turn off the oven," "lock the doors," and "call Mary."

Organize: Generally speaking, the better organized you are, the more likely you are to remember everything you need to remember. There are a variety of ways to organize. It may be beneficial to link the items you need to remember to a number. This works especially well if you have a short shopping list or if you need to perform tasks in a specific sequence. For example, if you have eight items on a grocery list, remember the number eight. Memorize both the numbers and the items. Or, at the office, you can number the tasks you hope to accomplish during the day and write that number in a bright color on your desk calendar as a reminder.

ESSENTIAL MEMORY TRICKS FOR EFFECTIVE RECALL

Have you ever gone into a room with a purpose clearly in mind only to forget why you went there? Often, if you return to the place where the thought originated, you will be able to recall what it was you went to get. This is called a *context-dependent memory*. When you experience problems with recall, focus on the context of the memory rather than on the content. Focusing exclusively on pulling out the memory will result only in frustration. In other words, focus on the journey of the recall process rather than the frustration about the destination. For example, if you can't remember the name of your boss's spouse, think about the contexts in which you met the person. Was it at a party? How were you feeling when you met this person? Do you remember what season it was? All of these clues will lead you back to the information you are trying to remember.

Similarly, it is frequently helpful to return to the same state of mind that you were in when you encoded the memory. If you were very happy when you created the memory, the memory is more likely to be accessible when you are happy. This is called a *state-dependent memory*.

Association: Another trick is to bypass the whole process of recall. Using association can help you do this. For example, if you place an empty egg carton on your car seat when you leave home to go to work in the morning, you are certain to remember to stop at the grocery store to pick up eggs on your way home.

Alphabetical association: If you forget an item you need to remember, run through the alphabet. For each letter of the alphabet, run through random words that start with that letter. It's likely that when you arrive at the letter of the alphabet that the word you are trying to remember begins with, you will recall the item you are trying to remember.

Chunking: This memory tool involves breaking a large amount of information into more manageable pieces or "chunks." One common example of chunking is telephone numbers. A local phone number is seven digits separated (chunked) by a hyphen. The first data set is a series of three numbers followed by a hyphen and then a second data set of four numbers. A verbal example might be breaking a grocery list into categories like produce, meat, dairy, frozen foods, and so forth. Chunking helps make information management a little bit easier.

PQ3RST: This memory tool is a little more complicated than the previous ones; however, it is very effective for organizing and remembering data that you read, watch, or hear. PQ3RST stands for Preview, Question, Read, Rehearse, Review, Summarize, Test. This tool can be especially helpful when you're reading a textbook, technical data, or instructions for assembling furniture. The idea is to familiarize yourself (Preview) with the subject (or drawing). Ask yourself (Question) what information may be relevant to watch out for in the material. Then Read, Rehearse, and Review the information. Repetition is the key to remembering this type of data. Then Summarize the important elements of the material, and finally Test your recollection of the material.

Effective rehearsal: Practice memorizing data by using different memory systems to encode the data. For instance, if you want to remember to buy peanuts at the store, say the word "peanuts" aloud, then picture yourself reaching for a bag of peanuts from the shelf at the grocery store. Finally, imagine yourself cracking open the peanut shell with your hands and popping the peanuts into your mouth. At that point, you will have created the memory in three mediums: verbal, visual, and motor, thereby increasing the likelihood of remembering to buy peanuts at the store.

Primacy and recency: As a rule, we tend to remember either the beginning or the end of a list more easily. If you are trying to remember a lot of information and have found that you remember earlier data or more recent data better, these tips might work for you. Take frequent breaks from the material you are trying to learn. Change the order of the material to more effectively take advantage of the primacy/recency effect. Move end material to the beginning and beginning material to the end. In other words, rotate the items on your list. Allow sufficient time to elapse during your breaks to take advantage of the primacy/recency effect.

HELPFUL TOOLS

Assisted memory: There are many memory-aid devices available to assist your memory for ordinary tasks. These aids can be as complex as you can handle (electronics) or as simple as paper and pencil. You can use a wall calendar to keep track of doctor appointments or important occasions. For this to be an effective tool, though, you must establish the habit of checking the calendar, perhaps before you go to bed and again when you wake up. If you use a Palm Pilot or PC-based calendar, set the alarm to remind you of important appointments.

Keep a running list of tasks, in the order of their importance. Scratch them off as you complete them. Or, if your list is in random order, highlight the most important or critical tasks.

Organize shopping lists by the order in which you will find the items in the store.

Use your answering machine as a memory tool. If you are away from home and suddenly remember something you need to do, call yourself and leave a message. You can also use a household timer to remind yourself to do a task, such as take your medication. Set the timer, and when it goes off, you will be reminded of this important task.

Spotting your car: Do you have difficulty remembering where you parked your car at the grocery store, mall, church, work, or elsewhere? Many cars look identical, and we've all spent some miserable, self-punishing time wandering around the mall parking lot, praying for some small sign that will guide us to our vehicle. Make your car stand out from others by tying a fluorescent ribbon to the antenna. You will locate your vehicle quickly and save yourself the embarrassment and frustration of wandering aimlessly around the parking lot searching for your car. (You can buy fluorescent ribbon at any home improvement store).

You may also want to try parking in the same general location whenever you are at a particular parking lot: at the end of a row, for example, or near a specific store or entrance. These simple tools can free you from the need to spend unnecessary energy on committing specific locations to your short-term memory by allowing you to rely on external aids instead.

NECESSARY MEMORY TACTICS

Your environment and state of health can have a tremendous influence on your ability to remember. Moreover, your mind-set is critical to your ability to remember.

> YOUR ENVIRONMENT AND STATE OF HEALTH
> CAN HAVE A TREMENDOUS INFLUENCE ON
> YOUR ABILITY TO REMEMBER.

Relax your mind and body: When you are tense or anxious, it is very difficult for your brain to focus on new information or recall existing data. Focus on your breathing. Slowly breathe in through your nose and exhale through your mouth. Gradually slow and deepen your breathing. Relaxing your mind and your body increases the energy your brain has to apply to encoding and retrieving memories.

HEALTHY LIFESTYLE

Your body and your brain require a healthy, balanced diet for peak performance. Be sure that you are supplying your body with the recommended daily allowance (RDA) of nutrients, vitamins, and minerals. If you don't know what foods to eat for this purpose, there are many books on the market dedicated to healthy eating. Include exercise in your healthy lifestyle. Exercise increases your metabolism and enhances your body's absorption of nutrients.

Limit alcohol and eat healthy: Another component of a healthy lifestyle is minimizing your intake of alcohol and drugs. It's also important to limit your consumption of salt, sugar, fat, and other empty calories. Increase your water intake. Adequate hydration helps balance sodium levels, increases mental alertness, and improves digestion, kidney function, and absorption of nutrients and medications. It is recommended that you drink six to eight 8-ounce glasses of water every day.

Get quality sleep: Getting adequate sleep is also an important aspect of a good memory. Like memory, sleep is a process, and a chronic breakdown in any part of that process results in an impaired memory.

Sleep cycles through five stages (some models use six stages, including wakefulness). The first stage is drowsiness, followed by stage 2, which is a period of light sleep. Stages 3 and 4 are considered deep sleep states. The fifth stage of sleep is called REM (rapid eye movement) sleep, and it is characterized by physiological changes. There is rapid movement of the eyes, and heart rate and respiration are accelerated. It is also theorized that memories are consolidated during this stage of sleep. This theory suggests that we relive memories in our dreams and thus create a record of events in our mind. Regardless of the validity of this theory, it is known that a lack of sleep impairs our cognitive abilities. If you have difficulty falling asleep or wake frequently during the night, you may want to discuss a sleep study with your physician.

Menopause and perimenopause: Fluctuating levels of estrogen and progesterone can impair your memory. Symptoms of perimenopause and menopause may include the following in addition to cessation of the menstrual cycle: hot flashes, irritability, memory loss, loss of bone density (osteoporosis), increased cholesterol, and risk of heart disease and colon cancer. Regardless of the cause of menopause (hysterectomy or the natural aging process), always consult your doctor for treatment of these symptoms. Estrogen replacement therapy can relieve these symptoms, including impaired memory function.

Males: Impaired cognitive functioning and visuospatial memory can result from testosterone (androgen) deficiency. Furthermore, prostate cancer, which affects one in five men in the United States, can negatively affect memory. Note that the treatment of these medical conditions, as well as the conditions themselves, can cause memory impairments.

Medical conditions: There is a seemingly endless list of medical conditions and medications (see chapter 7) that can impair memory functioning. Some of the more common conditions that affect memory functioning include heart conditions, hormone imbalances, cancer, diabetes, chronic obstructive pulmonary disease, kidney problems, vitamin and mineral deficiencies (particularly vitamin B_{12}), degenerative eye conditions, and changes in vision and hearing. If you have any of these conditions, it is essential for you to visit a physician regularly for checkups.

Environmental factors: Although highly unusual, it is possible that the exhaust fumes from your car may be impairing your memory; left unresolved, this can lead to permanent memory complications. If your memory difficulties come and go, or worsen after driving, and include headaches and nausea, you may want to have your car checked for an exhaust leak.

It's also possible that your home furnace may have a carbon monoxide leak. Memory loss from this type of exposure is more prevalent in the colder months, when the furnace is in use. You might want to purchase a carbon monoxide detector or hire a professional to check your furnace and gas lines for leaks.

Exposure to toxins can also result in cognitive impairments. Excessive molds and mildew have been known to cause cognitive impairment. Alcohol is the most common neurotoxin. Other toxins include paint, glues, fuels, oils, cleaners, and so forth.

Toxic exposures usually result in other acute physical symptoms, such as vomiting, headaches, and skin abrasions. Always wear protective gear (e.g., masks, gloves, coveralls), and work in a ventilated area when you are exposed to these types of toxins.

WRAPPING IT UP

Try out the different tips, tricks, tools, and tactics listed here and see which work best for you. It takes a healthy mind, body, and spirit to create and recall memories but the techniques we've presented here can help your memory along. Happy remembering!

CONCLUSION
Future Directions

*You are born with all of the brain cells that you will
ever have.*

New nerve growth is not possible in the brain.

The two statements above are long-standing misconceptions about the brain that recently have been proved inaccurate. Through careful and controlled study researchers have determined that the brain is a wonderfully complex organ that is growing and evolving with each thought. The interconnections of single neurons (believed to be more than one hundred million) serve as the roads for the chemical messengers (over fifty have been identified).

These chemical messengers are responsible for the lightning-fast transfer of information to a complex series of circuits. These circuits interconnect the more than thirty known regions of the brain that govern vision processing. Researchers have mapped the brain's overall functioning and have detailed the actual changes in neuronal connections after a new memory is made. (For more information, check out www.sparknotes.com/psychology/neuro/brain anatomy/section4.rhtml.)

The old comparison of the brain to an engine or even a computer has been replaced with innovative concepts of a parallel processing model. The complex architecture and vast circuitry of the brain are capable of processing a level of data transfer and system regulation that is truly mind-boggling.

Endless possibilities for maintaining and enhancing brain functioning come with this new knowledge. With knowledge comes power. The brain has demonstrated a level of plasticity that was never imagined previously. This means that even old brains can change and repair themselves and that this is an ongoing process. More important perhaps is the possibility that with this new knowledge we can influence the human brain's future. New techniques, drugs, herbs, and other strategies are constantly being developed and introduced. This is truly the age of the revelation of the brain.

In this book we've done our best to communicate the most direct and effective ways you can make some improvement in your memory. We hope that you take this information with you in your daily life, and that it makes a real difference. A better memory can improve your quality of life in enormous ways.

Good luck, and may your memories be happy ones.

References

Brenson, H. 1975. *The Relaxation Response*. New York: Avon.

Brinton, R. D. 2004. Impact of estrogen therapy on Alzheimer's disease: A fork in the road? *CNS Drugs* 18(7):405-422.

Broytman, O., and J. S. Malter. 2004. Anti-Abeta: The good, the bad, and the unforeseen. *Journal of Neuroscience Research* 75(3):301-306.

Burke, J. R., and J. C. Morgenlander. 1999. Update on Alzheimer's disease: Promising advances in detection and treatment. *Postgraduate Medicine* 106(5):85-86, 89-90, 93-94, passim.

Clinical Pharmacology. 2004. Goldstandard Multimedia. Version 2.11 (accessed July 18, 2004).

Devi, G. 2004. New York Memory and Healthy Aging Services. *FAQs on Women and Alzheimer's Disease.* Available at www.ny memory.org/menmemandmoo.html (accessed July 12, 2004).

Espeland, M. A., S. R. Rapp, S. A. Shumaker, R. Brunner, J. G. Manson, B. B. Sherwin, J. Hsia, K. L. Margolis, P. E. Hogan, R. Wallace, M. Dailey, R. Freeman, and J. Hays. 2004. Conjugated equine estrogens and global cognitive function in postmenopausal women: Women's Health Initiative Memory Study. *Journal of the American Medical Association* 291(24): 2959-2968.

Fanning, Patrick. 1994. *Visualization for Change.* 2nd edition. Oakland, Calif.: New Harbinger Publications.

Farlow, M. R., A. Hake, J. Messina, R. Harman, J. Veach, and R. Amand. 2001. Response of patients with Alzheimer's disease to rivastigmine treatment is predicted by the rate of disease progression. *Archives of Neurology* 58(3):417-422.

Finefrock, A. E., A. I. Bush, and P. M. Doraiswamy. 2003. Current status of metals as therapeutic targets in Alzheimer's disease. *Journal of the American Geriatric Society* 51(8):1143-1148.

Frautschy, S., W. Hu, P. Kim, S. A. Miller, T. Chu, M. E. Harris-White, and G. M. Cole. 2001. Phenolic anti-inflammatory anti-oxidant reversal of A(beta)-induced cognitive deficits in neuropathology. *Neurobiology of Aging* 22(6):993-1005.

Heyman, A., D. Schmechel, W. Wilkinson, H. Rogers, R. Krishnan, D. Holloway, K. Schultz, L. Gwyther, R. Peoples, C. Utley, and C. Haynes. 1987. Failure of long term high-dose lecithin to retard progression of early-onset Alzheimer's disease. *Journal of Neural Transmition* (Suppl.) 24:279-286.

Koltai-Attix, D., D. J. Mason, and K. Welsh-Bohmer. 2003. Neuropsychological consultation and training of family members of patients with dementia. In *Clinical Neuropsychology and Cost Outcome Research*, ed. G. Prigatano and N. H. Pliskin. New York: Psychology Press.

Krishnan, K. R., H. C. Charles, P. M. Doraiswamy, J. Mintzer, R. Weisler, X. Yu, C. Perdomo, J. R. Ieni, and S. Rogers. 2003. Randomized, placebo-controlled trial of the effects of donepezil on neuronal markers and hippocampal volumes in Alzheimer's disease. *American Journal of Psychiatry* 160(11): 2003-2011.

Le Bars, P. L., F. M. Velasco, J. M. Ferguson, E. C. Dessain, M. Kiesser, and R. Hoerr. 2002. Influence of the severity of cognitive impairment on the effect of the Ginkgo biloba extract EGb 761 in Alzheimer's disease. *Neuropsychobiology* 45(1): 19-26.

Maltby, N., G. A. Broe, H. Creasey, A. F. Jorm, H. Christenson, and W. S. Brooks. 1994. Efficacy of tacrine and lecithin in mild to moderate Alzheimer's disease: Double-blind trial. *The British Medical Journal* 308:879-883.

Mason, D. J. 2004. *The Mild Traumatic Brain Injury Workbook.* Oakland, Calif.: New Harbinger Publications.

Mason, D. J., and M. L. Kohn. 2001. *The Memory Workbook.* Oakland, Calif.: New Harbinger Publications.

Maxwell, C. J., D. B. Hogan, and E. M. Ebly. 1999. Calcium-channel blockers and cognitive function in elderly people: Results from the Canadian Study of Health and Aging. *Canadian Medical Association Journal* 161(5):501-506.

Mayeux, R., and M. Sano. 1999. Treatment of Alzheimer's disease. *New England Journal of Medicine* 341(22):670-679;

Niemann, H., R. Ruff, and C. Baser. 1990. Computer-assisted attention retraining in head-injured individuals: A control efficacy study of an outpatient program. *Journal of Consulting Clinical Psychology* 58:811-817.

Physician's Desk Reference. 2001. Thomason PDR: Montvale, New Jersey.

Preston, J. D., J. H. O'Neil, and M. E. Talaga. 1999. *Handbook of Clinical Psychopharmacology for Therapists.* 2nd edition. Oakland, Calif.: New Harbinger Publications.

Raskind, M. A., E. R. Peskind, T. Wessel, and W. Yuan. 2000. Galantamine in AD: A six-month randomized, placebo-controlled trial with a six-month extension. The Galantamine USA-1 Study Group. *Neurology* 54(12):2261-2268.

Reisberg, B., R. Doody, A. Stoffler, F. Schmitt, S. Ferris, and H. J. Mobius. 2003. Memantine in moderate-to-severe Alzheimer's disease. *New England Journal of Medicine* 348(14):1222-1241.

Sabiston, D. S., ed. 1997. Alzheimer's Disease. *Duke Medical Update* 4(1).

Schneider, L., and J. Olin. 1994. Overview of clinical trials of hydergine and dementia. *Archives of Neurology* 51(8):787-798.

Scott, H. D., and K. Laake. 2001. Statins for the reduction of risk of Alzheimer's disease. Cochrane Database Syst Rev. 2001; (3):CD003160.

Solomon, P. R., F. Adams, A. Silver, J. Zimmer, and R. DeVeaux. 2002. Ginkgo for memory enhancement: A randomized controlled trial. *Journal of the American Medical Association* 288(7):835-840.

Stankov, L. 1988. Aging, intelligence and attention. *Psychology and Aging* 3(2):59-74.

Sung, S., Y. Yao, K. Uryu, H. Yang, V. M. Lee, J. Q. Trojanowski, and D. Practico. 2004. Vitamin E supplementation in young but not aged mice reduces Abeta levels and amylodi deposition in a transgenic model of Alzheimer's disease. *The FASEB Journal* (2):323-325.

Tabet, N., and H. Feldmand. 2003. Ibuprofen for Alzheimer's disease. Cochrane Database Syst rev. 2003;(2):CD004031.

Thompson, T. L., C. R. Filley, W. D. Mitchell, K. M. Culig, M. LoVerde, and R. L. Byyny. 1990. Lack of efficacy of hydergine in patients with Alzheimer's disease. *New England Journal of Medicine* 323:445-448.

Yesavage, J. A. 1989. Techniques for cognitive training of memory in age-associated memory impairment. *Archives of Gerontology and Geriatrics* 1:185-190.

Douglas J. Mason, Psy.D., is a neuropsychologist who specializes in the diagnosis and rehabilitation of people with brain injuries and other cognitive disorders. He is currently in private practice in central Florida. His practice is called The Memory Doctor, LLC. To learn more, please visit him at www.thememorydoctor.com.

Spencer Xavier Smith is a freelance writer and editor based in Santa Rosa, CA.

Some Other New Harbinger Titles

Eating Mindfully, Item 3503, $13.95

Living with RSDS, Item 3554 $16.95

The Ten Hidden Barriers to Weight Loss, Item 3244 $11.95

The Sjogren's Syndrome Survival Guide, Item 3562 $15.95

Stop Feeling Tired, Item 3139 $14.95

Responsible Drinking, Item 2949 $18.95

The Mitral Valve Prolapse/Dysautonomia Survival Guide, Item 3031 $14.95

Stop Worrying Abour Your Health, Item 285X $14.95

The Vulvodynia Survival Guide, Item 2914 $15.95

The Multifidus Back Pain Solution, Item 2787 $12.95

Move Your Body, Tone Your Mood, Item 2752 $17.95

The Chronic Illness Workbook, Item 2647 $16.95

Coping with Crohn's Disease, Item 2655 $15.95

The Woman's Book of Sleep, Item 2493 $14.95

The Trigger Point Therapy Workbook, Item 2507 $19.95

Fibromyalgia and Chronic Myofascial Pain Syndrome, second edition, Item 2388 $19.95

Kill the Craving, Item 237X $18.95

Rosacea, Item 2248 $13.95

Thinking Pregnant, Item 2302 $13.95

Shy Bladder Syndrome, Item 2272 $13.95

Call **toll free, 1-800-748-6273,** or log on to our online bookstore at **www.newharbinger.com** to order. Have your Visa or Mastercard number ready. Or send a check for the titles you want to New Harbinger Publications, Inc., 5674 Shattuck Ave., Oakland, CA 94609 Include $4.50 for the first book and 75¢ for each additional book, to cover shipping and handling. (California residents please include appropriate sales tax.) Allow two to five weeks for delivery.

Prices subject to change without notice.